Raising Difficult Kids

Raising Difficult Kids

Stuart Passmore
BSc (Psych.), Honours (Psych.)

PAN

First published in Australia 2016 by Exisle Publishing Pty Ltd

First published in India 2016 by Pan
an imprint of Pan Macmillan India
a division of Macmillan Publishers India Private Limited
Pan Macmillan India, 707, Kailash Building
26, KG Marg, New Delhi – 110 001
www.panmacmillan.co.in

Pan Macmillan, 20 New Wharf Road, London N1 9RR
Basingstoke and Oxford
Associated companies throughout the world
www.panmacmillan.com

ISBN 978-93-82616-89-4

1 3 5 7 9 8 6 4 2

Typeset by Manmohan Kumar
Printed and bound in India by
Replika Press Pvt. Ltd.

To my wife and children, thank you
for all your patience and support.

To my father in heaven,
I dedicate this book to you.

Contents

Introduction

Parenting is perhaps one of the greatest rewards of human experience. The indescribable joy of being present at the birth of your child and holding that tiny and vulnerable little person in your arms for the very first time. The innocence of those big eyes staring deeply into yours, the big gummy smiles, the precious attempts at saying 'Dada' or 'Mama', and those special moments when they fall asleep in your arms or snuggle deeply into your neck. But for some, parenting can also be one of the most difficult 'jobs' in the world.

Some children just seem to be difficult right from birth. They are difficult to console when they get upset and they seem to resist every effort to comfort them. They have tantrums, they are defiant, they argue with you and demand their own way and continue to disobey you or completely ignore your instructions. They can steal from you, push you, hit you, run away, lie to your face and find themselves in trouble with the law. Sometimes a child's unusual and difficult behaviour is a result of developmental and behavioural disorders such as Autism

Spectrum Disorder, Oppositional Defiance Disorder or Attention Deficit–Hyperactivity Disorder.

But not every challenging child has a behavioural disorder; some children are just plain difficult, defiant and aggressive. Parents of such taxing children find that parenting can become very, very difficult. The constant strain and demands of parenting such children often places enormous stress on the parents. I can't tell you how many times I've heard parents tell me things like 'I hate my life', or 'I just can't take this any more', or 'I can't help but think if he wasn't in our life, things would be so much easier', or 'I walked out of the house this morning and I did not want to come back', or 'I've just called the police to deal with my child'. Sometimes parents find themselves in a state of desperation while trying to control their child's behaviour and they begin having thoughts that really scare them. Some parents have thoughts of hurting their children, others of abandoning their children, and still others of adopting or fostering their child out, while some parents have suggested that they would be happy to just fall asleep and never wake up again. This constant strain and desperation can often leave such parents feeling alone and isolated, believing that no one understands their situation and that they have no external support.

Raising Difficult Kids has been written with the intention of supporting all parents, but especially those parents who are at their wits' end and feel as though they have nowhere else to go. This book has been written with those parents in mind whose children have behavioural disorders, are defiant or who have explosive behaviours, or are just plain difficult to manage. It is based on the RANE® Parenting Program I developed over a number of years using the most up-to-date professional literature and research. As you read through this book, it is anticipated you will begin to realize just how important your parenting skills are for the well-being of your child and for maintaining a healthy relationship with your child. Unfortunately by the time most parents seek the professional help they need, the situation at home with their child has become, or is rapidly becoming, desperate. The parent–child relationship often begins to deteriorate with parents feeling powerless to alter their child's behaviour. This adds further strain in the home and can create a greater feeling of desperation for the parent.

Over the years many, many parents have sought my help and one of the things that is most evident to me is their vulnerability and their fear of being told what awful parents they are, how they have totally failed as parents, and of being blamed for their child's behaviour. According to the professional literature, various parenting styles have been found to underscore a deteriorating parent–child relationship and have also been directly linked to acting out, aggressive and delinquent behaviour in children. But one thing needs to be clear right from the start – this book is not about pointing the finger of blame. This book not only aims to provide current thinking on the issues of parenting but further seeks to unite a number of diverse disciplinary perspectives to provide an understanding of the parenting techniques, skills and strategies that are considered to be the most adaptive and functional, and that are most respectful of both the child and the parent.

Raising Difficult Kids is divided into two sections. Section 1 will begin to teach you appropriate and effective parenting skills and introduce you to the four most commonly accepted parenting styles. The purpose of this is to help you to honestly evaluate your parenting style. Understanding how you parent and then matching that to the most adaptive parenting techniques is often the beginning of change for many families. The remaining chapters in Section 1 explain how to develop new parenting skills while constantly building on the previous chapters. For some of you this will require radical changes to your parenting style and the way you typically respond to your child. Each chapter has accompanying homework to give you an opportunity to apply your new skills in a variety of situations.

Section 2 of the book is concerned with discipline. It is widely accepted in the professional world that harsh, punitive punishment is ineffective in modifying a child's problematic behaviour in the long term. The child will stop their misbehaviour in the short term but won't have 'learned the lesson'. Further, harsh punishment does not provide children with an appropriate reason to modify their behaviour; the unfavourable behaviour is likely to continue. There are some serious problems with corporal punishment that lie within the emotionally charged nature of the parent–child relationship in homes where the child's behaviour is difficult to manage. Simply put, it doesn't take much for an exhausted, stressed and angry parent who feels pushed to the edge to 'discipline' their child in anger. Unfortunately this 'discipline' is often harsh and punitive, and risks maintaining the child's problematic and/or aggressive behaviour.

We have all heard at one time or another that corporal punishment can and does lead to physical abuse. A parent lashing out at their child in anger also runs the risk of physically hurting their child. But what is not always so obvious is the potential emotional and psychological damage corporal punishment can do to a child. One teenage boy reported that when his mother was angry with him she would lash out and strike him in the face while screaming, 'You stupid, stupid boy!' According to the teenager he didn't remember the physical pain of being slapped in the face, but the words his mother screamed at him 'cut deep'. Is it any wonder that harsh, punitive punishment jeopardizes and damages the parent–child relationship and potentially causes more difficult behaviour from your child?

Effective discipline must include children receiving appropriate instruction and guidance for socially acceptable behaviour. Keeping this in mind, the chapter on discipline in Section 2 of this book is designed to teach you more adaptive and constructive ways of responding to your child's problematic and difficult behaviour. Section 2 also covers the complex issues of household chores, pocket money and the issue of rewarding children for their efforts and compliant behaviour. Principally, household chores are all about the child learning to take responsibility for themselves and becoming a responsible member of the family. As a member of the family unit, a child ought to learn to take on family responsibilities that also serve to support the unique needs of each family. As the original meaning for the term 'discipline' is 'to teach, to guide and to instruct', teaching a child how to become responsible is a natural part of discipline.

Let me encourage you to 'walk a mile in your child's shoes' to practise responding to your child with the respect and empathy you might expect from others. For instance, how might you feel about your spouse or partner if they lashed out in anger and hit you in the face while screaming 'You're stupid!'? We have a legal name for that type of behaviour today and it's 'domestic violence'. You will also notice that this book makes use of empathy on many occasions in order to help you build an understanding of your child's world and their unique experiences. It is important to understand that the questions posed in this book are not a judgment of you as a parent, but instead are neutral questions in order to help you understand your child's world.

As you read through this book you will find there are sections dedicated to the 'what to do when' or 'what to do if' questions. However, there is so much more to parenting than 'do this when this happens'. Parenting requires you to cultivate your own emotional intelligence so you can be secure, sensible, react calmly to a crisis and be there emotionally, psychologically and lovingly for your child. We all know that the way we were parented influences our own parenting styles and we also know that the way we were parented can leave us with incredibly happy memories. However, for some people, the memories of the abuse they suffered at the hands of their parents are something they desperately try to forget. As parents, we need to acknowledge our experiences of being parented to help us better understand how our children feel and how better to respond to them.

While it might be tempting to head straight to the chapters on discipline, I urge you to take the time to read the chapters on parenting first, as otherwise you may, in fact, risk increasing the problematic and aggressive behaviour in your child. Yes, you read that correctly. Your discipline measures could be making things worse. If you jump to the chapters on discipline in an effort to learn new ways of disciplining your child, that is all you will have learned. You have potentially neglected the most important responsibility you have: parenting. Parenting is not a right, it's a privilege – the greatest privilege we as adults can have. We are totally responsible for the life and the well-being of another person. Because parents are responsible for the whole child and not just their behaviour, you have a duty and a responsibility to do everything you can to learn how to be the best parent you can be. If your relationship with your child is not right, moving straight on to implementing new and improved ways to discipline them runs the risk of causing greater problems in your relationship and increasing bad behaviour. You will miss some of the most important principles in this book; namely that consequences are but one part, a very small part, of discipline.

Finally, this book has been written with an intended foundation of absolute respect for the child. It's a simple rule. Respect is earned and not automatically given because of your parental status. If you want your child to respect you, you must first learn to respect your child. For some parents this will go against everything you have believed and practised. But respect is a two-way street and children do need to learn to respect their parents and other people. The information in this book will help you teach your child about respect and will also help cultivate that attribute in your child.

FREQUENTLY ASKED QUESTIONS

Do certain types of parenting styles cause ADHD or Autism Spectrum Disorder?

NO! This is one of the most common myths I hear almost daily and it infuriates me. Parenting styles cannot cause these pervasive developmental disorders because ADHD, for instance, is a neurodevelopmental disorder. People who support such a myth really have no idea what they are talking about and they are certainly ignorant of professional research and the therapeutic interventions for these developmental issues. However, in saying that, certain parenting practices can increase angry, defiant, difficult and explosive behaviour and, in some circumstances, can also be the foundation for some behavioural disorders such as Oppositional Defiance Disorder. As you read through this book you will understand why.

Is this program strictly for parenting difficult children?

The short answer is no. This book has kept in mind those times when parenting can be exhausting, and sometimes parents don't know what to do in a variety of situations when dealing with a difficult child or teen. However, any parent wishing to further their parenting skills may benefit from reading this book as the skills and strategies can be adapted to children of virtually any age.

Individualizing the parenting management skills in this book

This book was never written with the 'one-size-fits-all' approach. While behavioural problems may have commonalities, no two families' experiences are alike. Just as each child is different and has a different personality, a different relating style and different needs, so must you be prepared to be flexible in your parenting style for each of your children. However, being flexible does not mean being a pushover and letting your children to do as they please. Flexible parenting means you will be mindful of each of your children's needs and will seek to use the various principles in this book that are relevant for each of your children.

Being flexible also extends to the pace at which you read this book and practise the principles. For instance, you may wish to complete one chapter and then take the time to practise the skills and principles before moving on to the next chapter. Remember that effective, healthy and adaptive parenting skills along with familial relationships take time to build; you can't expect an immediate change in the family, and you can't expect to have a new child in one week just because you have read a book on parenting.

MAINTAINING FOCUS

There have been occasions when parents undertaking this parenting program in my clinic have told me they were experiencing a lot of problems in their marriage, with quite a bit of conflict. It is well known that different parenting styles from each parent can cause huge problems in the marriage, and this has certainly been my experience. For instance, conflict often arises between the authoritarian and the permissive parent. The authoritarian parent blames the permissive parent for letting their child 'get away with everything', while the permissive parent believes the authoritarian parent is too harsh. In such cases, it's easy to see how this contrast in parenting styles can and often does create and maintain marital conflict. If this is the case, try to maintain focus on completing this book and *together* making the most of the principles discussed. One of the major goals of this program is to teach both parents how to work together and how to support each other in parenting roles, so that there is unison in your parenting.

Sometimes, though, the marital problems between you may be a major concern, leaving you feeling overwhelmed by the state of your relationship. If this is the case, you might benefit from seeking relationship therapy from an appropriately qualified and experienced professional (for example, a psychologist) to help you get your relationship back on track.

Why is discipline the last stage of this program?

Parents of children with behavioural disorders or children with explosive and defiant behaviours often tell me they have tried every kind of discipline they can think of to modify their child's problematic behaviour, without success. In some cases, the discipline has been severe enough for child protection departments or organizations to become involved with the family. Discipline can be misused by frustrated and angry parents who are at their wits' end. This defeats the purpose of a parenting book such as this one, where the ultimate goal is to teach you effective and appropriate parenting skills and to repair the parent–child relationship. However, if your child is engaging in risk-taking or dangerous behaviour, it is strongly recommended that you seek advice from a licensed and experienced professional (for example, psychologist, child psychiatrist, paediatrician or family doctor).

What should I do if I think my child might have a behavioural disorder?

If you think your child has a behavioural disorder (or any other disorder), it is strongly recommended you seek professional advice from the likes of a psychologist, child psychiatrist, paediatrician or your family doctor. An appropriately trained professional will have an understanding of both childhood behavioural disorders and pervasive childhood developmental disorders. This is a necessity, as there are a number of overlapping symptoms in pervasive childhood developmental disorders and behavioural disorders that require the clinician to have a thorough knowledge of diagnostic criteria to avoid incorrect assumptions and diagnosis. Not seeking qualified professional advice and support where needed may result in greater distress in the parent–child relationship and you might end up with an incorrect diagnosis.

When seeking professional advice always ask the individual to cite their qualifications and ask about their specific experience in parenting, family relations and childhood behavioural disorders. It is also important to ask the professional if they are registered by a professional board to practise; ask to see their registration certificate. Why would you ask these questions? In some countries, for example, anyone can decide to be a counsellor without having undertaken training or teaching of any kind. At worst this is potentially dangerous and at best it could be a waste of your hard-earned money to spend time with an individual who is not appropriately trained. A registered psychologist, on the other hand, must complete years of full-time training at university, is governed by a professional ethics board, and must continue ongoing training every year in order to retain their licence.

I'm divorced/separated. Will this program work for me?

The short answer is yes. Obviously it would be ideal if both parents took responsibility for parenting, and if that is the case, then the principles and strategies outlined in this book should be the same across both homes. This provides consistency, stability and routine for the child who knows what behaviour is expected at all times. However, there may be times when for whatever reason parents don't work together in their parenting responsibilities. The RANE® Parenting Program and this book have been designed to accommodate a variety of family circumstances such as single parenting, separation, divorce and foster care.

Section 1

DEVELOPING NEW PARENTING SKILLS

ONE

Belongingness and Attachment

A baby is born with a need to be loved – and never outgrows it. – Frank A. Clark

The Belongingness Hypothesis and Attachment Theory are two very prominent and powerful theories that have been influential and instrumental in shaping the foundation and application of this parenting program. The scope of these two theories is too large to discuss in detail, but it is essential to have a basic understanding of each of them.

The Belongingness Hypothesis has been applied to almost every aspect of our lives, including our need to belong to social groups, our need to belong to peer groups at school, at work, in spiritual groups and in society in general. It has also been applied to individual relationships and informs us of the significance of personal relationships in our overall well-being. The Belongingness Hypothesis argues that the need to belong is a fundamental human need and motivation, and that we have a pervasive and innate drive to form and maintain positive and significant relationships, even if they are only minimal ones. We are driven by a need to have frequent and emotionally pleasing interactions with a few select people or those who are incredibly important to us. Essentially, these interactions need to be free from persistent negative emotions such as anger, rejection and criticism, and negative conflict. Conflict is essential in healthy relationships, which might sound odd. But we all have arguments and, at times, an argument can clear the air and re-establish boundaries. Arguing can also have a healthy effect on a relationship. It's not that we can't argue; it's all about *how* we argue. You can argue with someone and still maintain respect for them. Negative conflict is damaging because it blames, attacks and undermines the other person in the relationship. The message conveyed is that 'there is something wrong with you' and 'it's all your fault', which is hurtful and can be incredibly damaging to any relationship.

Frequent and emotionally pleasing interactions need to be with the same people as often as possible, must be stable and should demonstrate an enduring and persistent care and concern for our well-being. We know that a lot of our behaviour, feelings and thinking processes are actually caused by or driven by this fundamental need to belong. When we feel as though we have very few meaningful relationships, we can experience an overwhelming sense of deprivation that can go well beyond just causing long-term emotional distress. As a result, people are at risk of developing anxiety, depression, grief, loneliness, relationship problems, instability, stress, behavioural and psychological problems, even health problems. Apply this to a child's need to belong that is not met and the effects can cause not only physical illness but also what is known as *psychopathology*, or severe mental illness, just as an adult would experience. Such deprivation can also be at the heart of behavioural problems and eating disorders, even suicide. It also appears that a great deal of maladaptive and destructive behaviour can develop out of a desperate attempt to form and maintain a close, secure bond or out of sheer frustration. If a child's need to belong is not met, a sense of worthlessness can develop.

However, when this need to belong is met, both adults and children are emotionally stable and therefore much happier. In fact, it seems that having a close and loving bond where the individual feels valued, needed, accepted and important is vital for our happiness. According to the Belongingness Hypothesis, our need to belong is not necessarily met by how much time (quantity) someone might spend with us, but by the quality of that interaction. Essentially what this means is that relationships that involve quality time combined with the expression of feelings of affection, understanding, closeness, tenderness and commitment go a long way towards fulfilling our need to belong.

ATTACHMENT THEORY

Attachment is one of those words that tends to get thrown around a lot and is used to describe so many different things. This means that the significant role of attachment when applied to the parent–child relationship can be misunderstood or underestimated. The parent–child attachment is one of the most important relationships in a child's life. It is so important that an unhealthy parent–child attachment can and does have life-long negative consequences for the child. But what is attachment and why is it important for the emotional and psychological health of the child? First, we really need to understand a little of the history of attachment or Attachment Theory. But before we do, there are a couple of things that need to be clarified. It seems a lot of the information about attachment really appears to be focused on the parent–infant or parent–toddler relationship or their attachment style. Those of you with older children might end up wondering if this material is relevant to you. You may even feel as if you have missed your chance or opportunity because you have older children. Don't worry. The principles of attachment remain the same regardless of the age of your child; it's never too late to start developing and maintaining a healthy and secure attachment with your child.

The concept of attachment styles was first introduced and pioneered by John Bowlby and Mary Ainsworth, who observed how children relate to their primary caregivers, which was usually the infant's mother. Bowlby is considered to be the founding father of Attachment Theory and he argued that the early mother–infant relationship (or other important carer) was very much one of the most significant predictors of a child's future personality development. After graduating from university in 1928, he undertook volunteer work at a school for dysfunctional and socially impaired children. It was during this time that two children left a lasting impression on Bowlby, becoming a pivotal influence on his decision to become a child psychiatrist. While he was studying medicine and psychiatry, Bowlby undertook further studies at the British Psychoanalytic Institute where he became convinced that family experiences were often the cause of an individual's emotional disturbance and that he could help children by helping their parents. In his very first empirical study, Bowlby completed a detailed analysis of case notes from

44 children who were described as having symptoms of being 'affectionless' and who had a 'tendency to steal'. Bowlby was able to link these symptoms to a history of maternal separation and deprivation when the children were young. After serving in World War II, Bowlby continued his work and argued that the dominant theories of the day (for example, Freudian) failed to adequately explain the significance of the mother–infant bond. Around this time, Bowlby came across a paper on animal imprinting written by Konrad Lorenz (1903–89), a zoologist who was one of the first people to describe the theory of attachment in geese and their hatchlings.

In what has become a classic experiment, Lorenz took the eggs laid by a Greylag goose and divided them into two groups. The first group of eggs was hatched by their mother and followed her around straight after hatching. The second group of eggs was placed in an incubator and after hatching they immediately followed Lorenz. The conclusion was that the hatchlings would accept as their mother whomever they first saw. Lorenz tested this further by separating the hatchlings from himself and their mother and placing them together in the same box. When he released them from the box, he found that the hatchlings would separate into the two groups and seek out either Lorenz or their mother. Although Lorenz was the first to coin the phrase 'imprinting', scientists later found that imprinting in a variety of bird species including ducks and geese happens between 12 and 17 hours after they have hatched. These observations led scientists to believe the notion that there are 'critical periods' during brain development and behaviour. Lorenz's experiments on the eggs directed the scientific community's attention towards understanding how early experiences can influence and shape social behaviour in adulthood. The theory of imprinting and the practice of naturalistic observations impressed Bowlby. From then on he began to apply the principles of ethology, as it helped him to expand the way in which he researched and theorized about mother–infant attachment.

After years of research and holding a number of very impressive positions, including being commissioned to write a report on the mental health of children after the war in Europe for the World Health Organization (WHO), Bowlby concluded that in order for the child to develop mental health they should experience a warm, loving, close relationship with their parents.

Mary Ainsworth also completed a university degree just before World War II broke out. During her studies at university, Ainsworth was exposed to the concepts of Security Theory, which essentially argued that infants and young children need to develop a secure dependence on their parents before they begin to explore unfamiliar surroundings. In her dissertation, Mary wrote: '*...where familial security is lacking, the individual is handicapped by the lack of what might be called a secure base.*'

Ainsworth moved to London, England, with her husband, where she applied for a research position under the direction of John Bowlby. Ainsworth was responsible for analysing data collected from naturalistic observations of children participating in the research project. She was so impressed with the rich information collected from the naturalistic observations of the children that she decided this approach would be included in any future research projects she undertook. Around 1956, Ainsworth collaborated on a paper with Bowlby, Boston and Rosenbluth that was very important to the development of Attachment Theory. Through her research and observations of children returning home after spending considerable time in a sanatorium, Ainsworth was able to classify three different types of relationships these school-aged children had with their parents. The three relationships included those with strong feelings towards their mothers, those who were obviously ambivalent about being reunited with their mothers, and those who were somewhat indifferent or hostile towards their mothers.

Mary and her husband moved to Uganda where she designed an observational research project on the development of mother–infant attachment. She was especially interested in the infants seeking closeness to their mother and when signals or behaviours were directed towards the mother to gain her attention. For about nine months, Ainsworth observed the infants in their home for two hours every two weeks. The results of her research found three infant attachment styles:

1. Infants classified as 'securely attached' hardly cried and were really quite content to explore their environment while their mother was nearby.
2. Those infants classified as 'insecurely attached' cried quite a bit, even if their mother picked them up and cuddled them. They were also quite reluctant to explore their environment, even if their mother was close by.
3. The final group of infants were classified as 'not-yet attached infants', showing no dependence on their mother.

The securely attached infants had mothers who were considered to be quite sensitive to the child's needs, while insecure infants were found to have mothers who were less sensitive to their needs. It was also found that infant security was related to the mother's enjoyment of breastfeeding their baby. These findings preceded Ainsworth's later and more sophisticated research on mother–infant attachment styles. However, the Ainsworths moved again and Mary's Ugandan research findings were put aside until she was once more in contact with Bowlby.

In 1963, Ainsworth embarked on what is considered to be one of the most significant and influential research projects on mother–infant attachment styles. Ainsworth had 26 families who joined the research project. She visited these families a total of eighteen times each in their home for a period of 4 hours each visit. While there were interviews taking place, this research project relied more on observing behavioural patterns of the parents and their babies in their natural surroundings. The home visits began during the infant's first month and ended when they were 54 weeks old. The project was huge and yielded an enormous amount of information. Essentially, the results showed typical mother–infant patterns of interactions developing over the first three months. For instance, Ainsworth observed quite pronounced differences between the mothers' sensitivity, appropriateness and how quickly they responded when their infants signalled for them. When mothers engaged in joyful play with their babies, the infants generally responded with happy or excited bouncing, smiling and vocalizing or otherwise expressing their happiness. But when mothers made face-to-face contact with their baby without talking to them and without smiling at them, the interaction between mother and infant was silent and brief. Mothers who were sensitive to their infants in those first three months tended to have a happier, more satisfied relationship with their baby at the 54-week period of the project. Infants whose mothers were caring and who tenderly held them and cuddled them in the first three months had babies who didn't need as much cuddling, but when they did seek close contact it was considered to be really quite satisfying and affectionate.

Ainsworth also conducted a laboratory research project known as the 'Strange Situation'. The project was originally designed to measure the level of attachment in one-year-old children when exposed to low- and high-stress situations. The mother and her baby were placed in a laboratory playroom and, at a later stage, were joined by an unfamiliar woman. The mother would leave the room for a short time and the stranger would play with the baby. Then the mother would return to the room. A second trial took place where the mother would leave the baby completely alone in the room. Again, after a short period of time, she would return to her baby, but this time with the stranger. While we would expect some of the findings, such as the baby feeling more secure playing with the toys in the presence of its mother, there were also some interesting and unexpected results. Ainsworth noticed that some infants were quite angry when their mothers returned. These one-year-olds cried and wanted close contact with their mother, but they would not snuggle in when she picked them up. Rather, these children were somewhat ambivalent towards their mothers and attempted to kick and hit out at them.

A second group of one-year-olds ignored or tried to avoid their mother when she returned to the playroom. Interestingly, these babies were actively seeking their mother when she had left the playroom. The research results revealed that the children who were ambivalent towards their mother or who tried to avoid her really didn't have the close, caring and sensitive relationship that the children who had a secure relationship with their mothers did. This laboratory project further supported Ainsworth's original classification of three distinct attachment styles and allowed further refinement of the three types.

So what does attachment mean? Simply put, children are born with an innate need and desire to form close, loving, secure, enduring and dependent bonds or relationships with their parents (or other significant caregiver) beginning from birth. Because of this driving need to form an attachment to the primary caregiver, they will do everything they can to form an attachment regardless of the quality of that attachment relationship between caregiver and infant.

As a result of all the research that has been done on attachment, a total of four attachment styles have been identified. One study that followed children from birth until they were six noted these attachment styles were still quite evident during this period. Today it is an accepted fact in the scientific community that these attachment styles are quite stable throughout the infant's and the child's life, and that the type of attachment formed in infancy/childhood can have quite serious implications for the adolescent and adult.

1. Secure Attachment

Securely attached babies and children don't like being separated from their parents, and when they are separated, they can protest about it quite strongly. When the parent returns, however, these children will actively seek out and try to re-establish that closeness with them and, if they have been crying, they settle pretty quickly when they are picked up or comforted by the parent. They also rely on and use their parent as a secure base to explore their surroundings, and if they feel anxious or worried while they are exploring or playing, they know their parent is close by to protect and support them and they can seek reassurance if needed. Securely attached children tend to be relaxed with their parent and will initiate enjoyable and pleasant interactions or respond quite positively when the parent initiates interaction.

2. Avoidant Attachment

Children that have an Avoidant Attachment style do explore their environment, but they tend to be unresponsive or uninterested in the parent who is with them. They keep their distance, make little eye contact and speak as little as possible to the parent by keeping busy playing with toys or by engaging in some other activity. They tend not to become distressed if the parent leaves their presence. In fact, they behave in such a manner that they ignore their parent's leaving and returning, and they tend not to snuggle in or cling to the parent when they are picked up. The Avoidant Attachment style is usually the result of a consistently inattentive, hostile or punitive parent who responds this way to the child when they are seeking safety, security or require needs to be met.

3. Resistant–Ambivalent Attachment

Children that are considered to be affected by Resistant–Ambivalent Attachment will display their preoccupation or fixation on seeking out their parent for closeness and comfort and really won't explore their surroundings. After being separated, however, they may want to seek out their parent but this infant tends to display angry and resistive behaviour and will hit out at and push their parent away, particularly when the parent tries to pick up their child. Also, these babies tend to cry even after being picked up as they are very hard to console and they are not easily soothed or comforted. While older children may still desire to be close to their parents, they continue to demonstrate avoidant behaviours such as turning their back while the parents are talking to them.

4. Disorganized–Disoriented Attachment

Finally, the Disorganized–Disoriented Attachment style is considered to reflect the greatest level of insecurity in the infant. It is all too commonly seen in children who have been maltreated by their parents (or significant caregiver). These children seem to be conflicted, as they simultaneously reach out for their parents and also turn away from them. This is because the infant or child is conflicted about the fact that the parent causes them an awful lot of distress and yet that parent is perceived as being their only source of comfort from distress. It is argued that the Disorganized–Disoriented Attachment style is most related to emotional distress and psychological illness. Older children try to control or direct their parent's behaviour by assuming a role one would expect to see from the parent. These children can accomplish this by humiliating or rejecting their parents with such statements as 'I told you to be quiet' or 'Leave me alone, don't bother me'. Other Disorganized–Disoriented children can appear to be overly considerate, caring and attentive or display a nervous excitement when the parent returns.

ATTACHMENT AND FATHERS

It is fairly evident that the history of attachment tended to focus on the mother–infant relationship with very little mention of the role or importance of father–infant/child attachment. This was primarily related to that time in history when the role of the woman was to stay at home, tend to the housework and raise the children while fathers were seen as the sole breadwinner. It's a good thing we are so advanced in our modern society that we have moved past these expected roles…

Fathers, regardless of your beliefs about what parenting is or what you have been told or even what you believe our culture expects of you as a man and a father, you have an incredibly critical role to play in the life of your child. These days it is a known fact that fathers also play an important role in their children's healthy psychological, emotional and social development. I know that many of you possibly do feel time pressured and have little time to spend with your child. But if I can be really blunt with you for just a moment: I don't care how busy you are. Your child needs you and it's simply not good enough to tell them 'I don't have time for you'. Imagine how devastated you would feel if your partner said that to you. Your child needs a stable, caring and competent father who goes far beyond the role of provider or disciplinarian. If you have time for a round of golf, you have time for your child. If you have time to meet your mates at the local pub or bar, stay back after work for a beer with colleagues or go to a local nightclub, you have time for your child. Sometimes significant decisions have to be made in order to include your child in your life. It's also not simply about how much time you spend with your child, it's about *how* you spend that time with them.

It has been my experience that the way in which a man defines his role as a father often influences his parenting behaviour. Although men can feel pressured to behave in a particular way with their children, they can engage with them on many different levels, such as teaching and playing with them, and being involved in the day-to-day caretaking. Essentially, the more a man sees the importance of his role as a father, the more involved with his children he is likely to be. This is also the case when separation or divorce takes place. The importance of the father in a child's life doesn't change or alter in any way just because the marital relationship is over. It seems a father can fall into the belief that because a separation or divorce has taken place, the fathering role or responsibility towards his children is somehow different. The simple answer is no, it is not. In fact, your child needs you to maintain your competent, caring and supportive role during this time. Parents constantly arguing, separating and divorcing is a time that is frightening for children. They don't need to contend with feeling abandoned by you because you have left the family or started a new relationship.

The father–child attachment is also understood to begin at birth, but I believe a father can begin to form an attachment to their baby even before that. Fathers can become involved in learning about the stages of the baby's growth *in utero* (in the womb). You can read books, magazines and articles about the different stages of growth and development of your unborn child. You can search the internet and attend the prenatal classes, you can talk with your partner about each stage of the baby's development. For instance, we know unborn babies at different stages of development are able to see, hear, taste, recognize voices and react with alarm to outside events such as noise and are receptive to what is happening in their mother's life. Some recent research has even found that unborn babies form memories at a subconscious level. So what all this means is that your unborn child actually begins to form a relationship with the external world, especially with their parents. It is for this reason that I encourage men to regularly put their head on the mother's stomach and talk to their unborn baby.

Your newborn baby needs you to talk to them, to pick them up and cuddle them, to kiss them, to smile at them and to play those exciting games with them. Your child needs you to be their companion, someone who will take care of them, be an honourable partner to their mother, someone who will protect them, guide them, teach them, be an appropriate model to them, and someone who is not afraid to teach them morals. Children need and desire to form a secure attachment to their father and this requires you to be sensitive to your child's needs and not just (as many mothers have described their husbands) the sperm donor. Whatever you do, don't buy into the old myth that women are 'biologically prepared' to be better caregivers to their children than men. Single fathers all over the world are demonstrating that they can be just as nurturing, caring, supportive, loving and protective of their children.

ATTACHMENT AND EMOTIONAL AND MENTAL HEALTH

There used to be a prominent theory floating around that children are resilient; that they can bounce back from almost anything. If a child was maltreated or traumatized, the potential damaging effects of such incidents weren't taken too seriously as the child would simply bounce back from it and everything would be okay. This is a load of rubbish. One thing I tell every parent who enrols in my parenting course is simply: 'What you say to your children today and how you treat them today will matter tomorrow!'

Think back to your own childhood and think about the hurtful things your parents said or did to you. The mere fact that you can remember these events and still experience those hurtful or painful memories and feelings is proof of their impact. But there can be far more serious implications than just some painful memories. The type of parent–child attachment style can have an effect on interpersonal relationships, mental health and also dictate the level of emotional distress felt by an individual.

Knowing that attachment is really concerned with the protection, care and perceived security of the child places the parent in the prime position of responsibility for developing a secure attachment with their child. Further on, you will read about the detrimental impact on the child's life that a poor parent–infant/child attachment can have. However, it is important to understand that insecure or poor attachment is not necessarily going to determine serious mental health problems in your child. Also, for the sake of ease, rather than continuing to list each of the attachment styles (Avoidant: showing disinterest in the parent, indifference to the parent's presence; Resistant–Ambivalent: showing angry and resistive behaviour and striking out at parents; Disorganized–Disoriented: very conflicted child and most related to emotional distress and psychological illness; and Secure: secure, non-anxious, happily engaging in a relationship with their parents), I will use just the terms 'unhealthy attachment' and 'secure attachment'. Finally, when you read the following information be aware that *both* the mother and father's attachment style to their children can influence the development of your child.

Association between insecure attachment and mental health

Children and adolescents who have experienced insecure attachment can often have issues with mental health. Studies have revealed the following:

- Five- to six-year-olds with an insecure attachment are typically less liked by peers and teachers.
- Children are considered to be more aggressive by their peers.
- Children are considered by their teachers to be less competent and have more behavioural problems.
- The quality of parent–child attachment in fifteen- to eighteen-year-olds has been found to be related to their development of social skills. Social skills are related to the individual's ability to successfully manage friendships and romantic relationships and communication skills, how they solve interpersonal problems and how they regulate their emotional responses to frustrating situations.
- The lack of social skills is related to a number of mental illnesses including depression, conduct disorders and social phobia.
- The affected development of social skills includes higher levels of depression. By the age of fifteen, girls are at twice the risk of boys to have suffered depression.
- Depression during adolescence is all too often associated with a number of very serious outcomes including intense feelings of loneliness and isolation, academic problems and a higher risk of repeated suicide attempts.
- Developing depression during childhood or adolescence also significantly increases the chances of your child developing psychological disorders in adulthood, such as anger being a prevalent emotion, higher levels of anxiety, developing phobias, externalizing behaviours such as aggression, damaging property, truancy and substance abuse.

- There is a strong association between Borderline Personality Disorder and insecure attachment.
- There is an association between attachment insecurity and physical illness such as a susceptibility to stress.
- There are links between insecure attachment and hyperactivity.
- Children have difficulty trusting others.
- There can be poor interpersonal relationships and difficulty in maintaining relationships in adulthood.

MOTHER AND FATHER'S ATTACHMENT STYLE AND NEGATIVE INFLUENCES ON SONS AND DAUGHTERS

Following is a brief list of negative influences that can occur in relation to the mother or the father's attachment style. What is obvious is that parental characteristics and attachment styles are related to aggressive externalizing behaviour in both sons and daughters.

- A mother's caregiving behaviour is a strong predictor of aggressive and disruptive behaviour in boys more than girls.
- Girls can be very susceptible to disruptions in family relationships.
- It is also known that a mother's level of hostility and aggression towards her daughter is strongly associated with the daughter developing a very serious behavioural disorder called Conduct Disorder.
- Fathers generally have a greater role in their sons developing externalizing behaviour (for example, aggression) than do their mothers.

Here are a few examples of the emotional and psychological distress as a result of poor parent–child attachment that I hear and see all too often in my clinic.

'I cried every day when I was a child because there was no love from my parents. I had lots of aunties around me but they were angry with me because I was crying. I guess I wasn't good enough to be loved.' ***(37-year-old male)***

'My mother gave me up when I was two years old … I don't know how to trust people and I don't know what they mean. I take everything as though they are attacking me and I don't know how to deal with it or change it. It has such an impact on me that I get really angry and reject the people in my life that are most meaningful and treat them very poorly.' ***(45-year-old female)***

'When he was just two years old his mother used to call him over to her and when he came she would literally push him away, scream obscenities at him and call him all sorts of names. She was so rejecting of him and said such cruel things to him that Child Services removed him from their home … Today he doesn't trust anyone. He won't allow you to get close to him, you can't touch him and he is always angry.' ***(The foster parent of fifteen-year-old boy)***

'I've tried to commit suicide 25 times. I've tried electrocution, I've tried to hang myself and pills … because my mother has always told me I'm fat and ugly.' ***(Sixteen-year-old girl)***

It's not a pretty picture, particularly when you remember that these issues can follow your baby or child for the rest of their life. Hopefully, you're beginning to realize how important your parenting style is.

Association between secure attachment and mental health

Following is a brief list outlining the benefits of developing a secure attachment with your children. They will:

- Have a healthy self-esteem.
- Be better able to regulate emotions in childhood and adolescence. Learning to regulate emotions is one of those healthy skills that protects teenagers and adults from developing depression.
- Gain social competency in childhood and adolescence.
- Have more adaptive coping strategies (coping strategies are broadly defined as problem- and emotion-focused strategies). Problem-focused strategies are about taking personal control in the face of challenges, accurately assessing the problem, and developing a plan of action that will reduce personal distress. Emotion-focused strategies usually involve the individual expressing their emotions and changing their expectations as necessary.
- Coordinate attention, feelings and behaviour far better as teenagers.
- Achieve academic motivation in adolescence.
- Tend to score more highly on intelligence tests and exams. They will also develop healthy study skills as they set and stick to their study goals.
- Adjust to high school and university more easily than those not so securely attached to their parents.
- Be more popular with their peers.
- Be able to control their emotions.

- Have a greater belief in helping others and a greater satisfaction with life during adolescence.
- Have lower levels of depression and anxiety.
- Be less likely to be involved in crime compared with the statistics for insecurely attached children involved in crime. There will be significantly reduced violence, aggression, antisocial and delinquent behaviour.
- Be less likely to experience emotional distress or to attempt suicide.
- Display evidence of significantly reduced drug and alcohol use and abuse.

MOTHER AND FATHER'S ATTACHMENT STYLE AND POSITIVE INFLUENCES ON SONS AND DAUGHTERS

Following is a brief list of positive influences that can occur in relation to the mother or the father's attachment style.

- Father–child secure attachment is related to lower conflict in bestfriend relationships.
- Mother–child and father–child secure attachment is significantly related to higher self-worth.
- Perceptions of one's self-worth are related to social competence. Mother–child and father–child secure attachment is also significantly related to social competence.
- Self-worth is related to a lesser chance of developing anxiety and feelings of rejections from others.
- A healthy sense of self-worth significantly reduces the risk of the child becoming aggressive.

Now that you understand the importance of developing a secure attachment with your child, it's easy to see how what you say to your child and how you treat them today will matter tomorrow. The following chapters are designed to begin teaching you how to develop a secure attachment with your child. The next step is to learn about the different parenting styles that either promote or damage the parent–child relationship.

TWO

Four Different Parenting Styles

We must do what is right for our babies, long term for our families. – Laurel Wilson

I remember a time when you walked into a major retail store and you could see a business statement, corporate vision or slogans pinned to the walls for all the customers to read, letting them know of the business's commitment to making their customers happy. Successful businesses usually don't just spring up out of nowhere to become an overnight success. Sometimes years of planning and preparation take place before a business can begin. And without constant planning and forward thinking, a business is destined to collapse in a relatively short period of time.

The business model is a useful analogy, as we can look at parenting in a similar way. If you ask parents about their vision for their child, or what their desired future or projected growth will be five years from now, the common theme that runs through the majority of parent responses is simply one of parents wanting to have a close relationship with their children; for their children to feel they could approach them at any time and talk with them about any problems. I have heard very few parents describe in detail their family vision, their projected growth for their family, or even a family statement, let alone outline detailed planning and preparation to meet their goals, dreams or desires as a family. My point is that, just as you would plan for a business to develop and grow, so these principles also apply to building a secure, happy and close-knit family. It takes many years of planning and commitment and will not happen overnight.

Keeping with the business analogy, a company divided against itself will not survive. If all the stakeholders are at odds, nothing will happen and the business will eventually disintegrate. The same principle applies to families: each member of the family must work with all of the others both individually and together for the good of the family unit.

Parents need to be aligned in their parenting efforts and present a unified front, working towards the goals and dreams they have for their family. And this can be tricky, as people tend to parent the way they were parented and rarely question their own parenting style.

If parents have different parenting styles and don't parent in a partnership (this is called interparental conflict), this often leads to arguing about the differences in parenting and will more often than not leave one or both parents feeling isolated and ill-supported in their efforts. Eventually the different parenting styles can become a point of conflict. The conflict 'leaks' out into the marriage and marital conflict develops. So now the parents are not only arguing over differences in parenting styles, but as husband and wife they also begin to argue about anything and everything. Take for instance the following report from a father:

> *'My wife is permissive. The kids know if they push her hard enough they can get away with anything. But they know they can't with me. I make them do as they're told. And I'm the one who punishes them. Now I'm the bad guy because I have to do all the punishing. My wife doesn't like the way I punish them and we're always arguing over how she lets the kids get away with anything … Now we just seem to be arguing all the time.'*

But perhaps more disturbing is the fact that couples arguing over their different parenting styles can actually find their marriage dissolving and ending in separation and divorce. On the other hand, we also know that when parents are operating from the same page in their parenting efforts they tend to get along much better. The marriage relationship is secure. In these homes, it has been shown that children will also feel safe and secure. Yes, you read that right. There are very strong associations between the state of a marriage and a wide range of childhood behavioural and emotional problems.

Marital therapists would be well aware of the many times when parents have presented for marital counselling and told the the therapist of their concerns about their children's difficult behaviour. I often find that as the couple work through marriage counselling and begin rebuilding their relationship, I also begin to hear more and more about how the child's difficult behaviour is decreasing.

Take for instance a middle-aged couple who came to see me for marital counselling. During the early stages of counselling they told me about their teenage daughter's rebellious behaviour and the way in which she ignored all the boundaries they set for her. If the parents confronted their daughter regarding the way in which she blatantly broke the rules, an argument would break out. Both parents were becoming increasingly frustrated. However, as the parents progressed through the relationship counselling and began focusing on rebuilding their relationship, they began to report a noticeable difference in their daughter's behaviour. While their daughter was still disregarding their rules, they noticed that when she came home from a night out, rather than ignoring them and locking herself in her bedroom, she was beginning to spend more time with them just sitting and talking. As time passed the parents reported that their relationship with their daughter was undergoing some major improvements and they were now able to calmly sit and discuss their concerns about her behaviour and set boundaries.

By learning about your parenting style you can begin to bridge the gap with your spouse if you find you each have different parenting styles. This will allow you to begin the process of parenting in unison and will begin to establish a foundation of mutual parental cohesiveness, and support and respect for each other, rather than feeling like you are each working against the other. The following section introduces you to the four parenting styles. Take note of each style and decide which one describes you best. Some parents have said they can see themselves in two of the parenting styles. You might even think that not one of them is totally you. That's okay, the point here is to try to recognize what characteristics or attitudes or behaviours you might identify with most. You may not be as harsh as the authoritarian parent or as relaxed with rules as the permissive parent, but you may recognize or identify with certain characteristics of one of the styles.

These four parenting styles have been taught in books and parenting seminars and workshops under different names. Whatever the name, the characteristics are fundamentally the same. Keep in mind, too, that the parenting styles presented are indicative of extreme cases of each of the negative styles. This is deliberate, as I want to show you the harmful and damaging effects that some parenting styles can have on children. It might be helpful for you to think of each of the four parenting styles as a continuum. For instance, the extreme end of the authoritarian parenting style lacks any expression of warmth, is harsh, demanding and will often resort to force and punishment in order to achieve conformity from the child. While the less 'extreme' authoritarian parent may express some warmth toward the child, they may continue to suppress the child's self-expression and use harsh punishment, at times, to achieve conformity.

AUTHORITARIAN PARENTING

Authoritarian parenting is described as hostile because these parents use a high degree of control and monitoring, and are generally poor at nurturing their child or showing warmth. They are characterized by strict, inflexible rules. Some of the key traits of these parents are listed below.

- They have a high degree of control over their children and may monitor their children's whereabouts and their activities to a repressive degree, but tend to lack warmth and nurturing qualities.

- These parents will avoid their children if they do not meet their own expectations or they will tell their children they are not as good as others, either directly or through their behaviour.
- They have a belief that if their children fail to conform to their requests, the children may be deliberately attempting to undermine the parents' authority.
- They believe parental power is automatically legitimized by their position in the family.
- They place too high a value on conformity.
- The rules and demands placed on their children generally suit the parents at that particular moment.
- They are demanding on all levels.
- They use power-assertive practices and are low in responsiveness to the child and their needs.
- This style of parenting can also reject the children when they are unwilling to obey. The premise here is 'Do it because I say so'.
- They ignore, tend to be uninterested, belittle and get little enjoyment out of their children.
- These parents engage in very little give and take with children, who are expected to accept an adult's word in an unquestioning manner. This authoritarian style is biased towards the parents' needs, suppressing the children's self-expression and independence.
- If children fail to conform, authoritarian parents often resort to force and punishment to ensure the children conforms to their demands. This style of parenting often uses corporal punishment, shaming and manipulation to achieve their demands of the children. This can leave the

children in the family feeling insignificant and powerless. This is sometimes expressed with anger and aggression (especially in boys).

Take a moment to ask yourself the following questions:

1. Does it appear that this parenting style would be very effective? Why or why not?
2. How do think this parenting style might impact your child?
3. Why would a child parented in this way tend to show more anger and aggression?
4. What do you think might be the immediate and long-term social and emotional consequences for a child (for example, interpersonal difficulties, relationship difficulties, employment difficulties)?
5. Why do you think that might occur?
6. What are the potential immediate and long-term educational implications for a child living in an authoritarian home?

Listed below are the effects this type of parenting can have on children.

- Preschoolers with authoritarian parents were found to be anxious, withdrawn and unhappy. Boys, especially, tend to show higher rates of anger and defiance, while adolescents are more likely to be less well adjusted.
- In general, children are more likely to develop low self-esteem, are generally unhappy, discontented, withdrawn and mistrustful.

- This style of parenting has been positively correlated to aggressive behaviour in children.
- Boys growing up with this parenting style are far more likely to develop behavioural problems.
- This type of parenting is linked to a severe behavioural disorder known as Conduct Disorder.
- Critical, rejecting parents increase the likelihood of children avoiding emotional intimacy. The children from these families are deficient in developing empathy and social skills. There is also a negative effect on a child's self-concept.

The importance of self-concept

Parents and families are considered to be crucial to their child's developing self-concept. Professionals argue that a parent's relationship with their child has the potential to significantly influence their child's sense of self-worth and self-confidence.

Put simply, parents have an enormous influence over their children's developing self-concept and emotional calmness. The same researchers explained self-concept as confidence and self-worth while emotional calmness has been defined as calmness, freedom from anxiety and depression. Children with low self-concept can:

- Be less co-operative.
- Be less persistent on tasks.
- Have poor leadership abilities.
- Be at greater risk of developing anxiety.
- Can have a negative attitude toward school, really aren't expecting to achieve academic success and have low academic ambitions.

- Have less positive friendships compared to children of similar age.
- Have an external locus of control (tend to blame others for their behaviour rather than accept responsibility for their actions).

Psychological control

Psychological control is a particular behaviour that is commonly associated with the authoritarian style of parenting and has been described as: *...control attempts that intrude into the psychological and emotional development of the child (for example, thinking process, self-expression, and attachment to parents)* (Barber 1996).

Psychological control is very different to behavioural control. Behavioural control is really about the parent regulating their child's behaviour by means of setting limits and monitoring what their children are doing. In contrast, psychological control uses various means of pressure to have your child comply with your demands. These kinds of tactics would include creating a feeling of guilt in your child, shaming your child, and withdrawing your love and affection from your child (for example, giving your child the silent treatment). So love, acceptance and parental warmth become conditional and are only given if your children comply. This is ultimately self-serving and is a way of manipulating and exploiting the parent–child relationship.

While it is probably fair to say that not all parents are aware they might be using psychological controlling tactics, such methods tend to pressure children into compliance. Those children who have been at the raw end of parental psychological control have been found to develop a number of behavioural and psychological problems during childhood and adolescence. For instance, psychological control has predicted:

- Increases in the child internalizing problems, leading to mental health problems such as anxiety and depression in childhood and adolescence.
- Increased risk of developing stress and low self-esteem. In boys it is also responsible for a decrease in self-confidence.
- Increased risk of a child developing behavioural problems such as acting out and aggressive behaviour and childhood delinquency.
- A drop in school grades and a decrease in psychosocial maturity (both psychological and social maturity).
- That the child has an increase in complaints of illness or symptoms resembling an illness.
- That children growing up in such homes are consistently found to have unreasonable and quite often unfounded feelings of guilt. They are typically dependent, alienated, socially withdrawn, have an inability to make a conscious choice or decision and are passive and inhibited.
- It can represent a threat to the child's developing sense of self.

Psychological control is a far cry from a healthy, balanced form of parenting that nurtures a child's expressions and opinions. Such parenting rarely responds to a child's emotional and psychological needs as it tends to supress a child's naturally developing autonomy and individuality, leaving no room for verbal give and take between parent and child.

However, psychological control is not the only form of control an authoritarian parent will use. Excessive parental control has been defined as a set of behaviours where parents typically use excessive control to regulate their child's activities and routines. This form of excessive control actively encourages the child to develop a dependence on the parents rather than allowing the child to naturally develop their own sense of self and autonomy. These parents will also instruct their children on what to think and how to feel. This is very different to guiding, explaining and teaching a child about emotions or thoughts about an event or even how they may express themselves.

In my experience, many authoritarian parents have argued their right to practise corporal punishment. For instance, when introducing this session on parenting styles, one mother angrily stated 'What's wrong with spanking the kid? I got spanked as a child and I turned out all right. That's the problem with society today; if more children got smacked there wouldn't be so much crime. I don't see anything wrong with spanking. I'm the authority here, and she needs to know who's in charge.' (This from a mother of a seven-year-old girl.) It is important to understand that corporal punishment only changes the child's behaviour right then and there. It is highly unlikely the child will internalize any moral message such as 'learning a lesson' from corporal punishment and, as such, the inappropriate behaviour is likely to remain unchanged in the long term. Furthermore, given the authoritarian parenting style it is quite probable any corporal punishment is likely to be done out of anger and frustration. You need to be aware of the potential message this is sending your child: when you're angry it's okay to hit someone. There is also the real and terrifying risk that a child can be badly harmed physically, too.

PERMISSIVE PARENTING

Typically there are two different types of permissive parenting. The first is identified with low monitoring of the child's whereabouts, low monitoring of the company they may keep, and low monitoring of their activities coupled with low control over the child's behaviours. That is, the parents avoid placing demands or controls on their children and avoid setting behavioural boundaries for their children. However, this type of permissive parent is typically very warm and nurturing of the child. The second type is characterized by poor monitoring of the child's whereabouts, low monitoring of the company they may keep, and low monitoring of their activities together with little or no love and affection, affirmation and acceptance. These permissive parents are characterized by little or no limit setting coupled with unpredictable parental harshness. However, it is important to point out that the second style of permissive parenting can, at times, be nurturing and responsive. Again, this type of parent avoids placing demands or controls on their children and they avoid setting behavioural boundaries for their children. Children are not taught fundamental social skills, impulse control, social etiquette rules and boundaries, nor are they taught conformity to both social and legal expectations.

Permissive parents allow children to make many of their own decisions when they are not developmentally mature enough to take on the responsibility. For example, I've met parents who allowed their ten-year-old son to choose whether he would go to school each day. Research indicates that permissive parenting is a result of many parents lacking the confidence in their own ability to influence their child's behaviour.

Children need friendly parents or parents who are caring, loving, supportive and who are willing to set boundaries if they are to thrive. They do not need parents to *be* their friends. If you are trying to be your child's best friend then you are doing them a disservice and there is a very good chance your motives are not as pure as you might like to believe. My experience has been that those parents wanting to be their child's friend are not always doing it for the child's benefit or for some other noble reason as they might have me believe. Instead, I have found their motives are much more self-serving: parents are afraid or even terrified that if they impose restrictions and enforce behavioural boundaries in their home, their child may stop loving them. For example, a middle-aged couple arrived at my clinic seeking marital counselling. The couple reported they had been arguing for years and during this time the arguments had become more and more frequent and were really quite hurtful. Their relationship was deteriorating and they were considering divorce. As the first session unfolded I could see what they meant by hurtful arguments. They made accusations and counter-accusations about each other, they yelled and screamed at each other, then the swearing and the name calling set in. At the end of it all, it came down to one thing – this was the woman's second marriage and she had a teenage daughter to her first husband. Her second husband believed he was excluded from forming a family relationship with his wife and stepdaughter as the wife seemed more interested in being friends with her daughter. The wife confirmed this. The husband further reported that before they were married they had discussed discipline and boundaries and some rules for her daughter. He believed the married couple's bedroom should be off limits to the daughter. He felt the bedroom represented privacy for the newlyweds and was a kind of sanctuary for him at the end of the day, a place where he could go to relax. However, any rules they had agreed on regarding discipline and boundaries with the daughter were not maintained by the mother. He believed as the stepfather of a teenage girl it was not his right to attempt to discipline her; rather it was the responsibility of her mother. However, as the mother would not discipline her daughter his frustration grew until conflict between the parents became extreme. He believed children should have rules and boundaries and be made to follow them. His wife said she was terrified that if she was to place rules and boundaries on her daughter that her daughter would hate her and that she would lose the love of her only child.

And another example. A number of years ago a 50-something-year-old man contacted my clinic and desperately pleaded with me to be seen immediately. When he arrived at my clinic he was visibly upset and really shaken. He told me he had arrived home from work a little earlier than usual to witness his 21-year-old son push his mother into the kitchen wall in a fit of anger. The father rushed over to assist his wife and then his son turned towards his father and showed aggression towards him. With a single blow to the face, the father knocked the son to the ground and, sitting on his chest, was about to begin punching his face when the son broke down in tears and begged his father not to hit him. This whole experience left both parents distressed and unsure of how to manage their son's behaviour. The following week both parents attended my clinic and as we talked the mother revealed her son had been verbally abusing her for some time and was becoming more and more aggressive towards her and had even threatened to punch her in the face. It wasn't long before the couple starting arguing and, sure enough, it emerged that they were angry at each other over their different parenting styles. The father angrily stated that as far back as he could remember his wife never 'made [the son] do anything. He could get away with anything and it was always me who had to discipline him, then she would get upset with me'. The mother admitted she was terrified of losing her son's love and that she would do anything for him to ensure he would continue to love her. Sadly, when I informed her she needed to learn to put some behavioural limitations on her son, she told me she would not do it as he might stop loving her. She never returned to my clinic.

So, for the record, permissive parents can also be overly tolerant and indulging. This type of parenting can promote a feel-good attitude regardless of how their child is behaving. Unfortunately, this tends to create a false sense of self-esteem, which can be harmful to a child's overall development. There is also a tendency for parents who constantly second guess themselves and are afraid to make the tough decisions to be, in turn, seen by their children as weak, incompetent parents. Such parents are rarely respected by their children.

WHAT ABOUT THE EFFECTS ON THE CHILDREN OF PERMISSIVE PARENTS?

Children of permissive parents generally:

- Are very immature and tend to have difficulty controlling their impulses (because there are no controls or boundaries).

- Have a tendency to be disobedient and rebellious when requests are made of them that conflict with their desires.
- Are likely to be overly demanding and dependent on adults.
- Show poor persistence on tasks generally. It is in preschool that the poor persistence becomes evident.
- Will less likely commit to sustained effort, which may explain why such children exhibit non-achieving, dependent behaviour, which is especially strong for boys.
- Can, as adolescents, exhibit poor self-control, with teenagers being less involved in school learning and more likely to be involved in substance abuse.
- Tend to be aggressive. The risk of the aggression increases towards those imposing rules on the child.

Take a moment to ask yourself the following questions.

1. Does it appear this parenting style would be very effective? Why or why not?
2. How do think this parenting style might impact your child?
3. Why would a child parented in this way tend to show more anger and aggression?
4. What are the potential immediate social and emotional implications for a child living in a permissive home?
5. What do you think might be the long-term social and emotional consequences for this child (for example, interpersonal difficulties, relationship difficulties, employment difficulties)?
6. Why do you think that might occur?

7. What are the potential immediate and long-term educational implications for a child living in a permissive home?

UNINVOLVED PARENTING

The uninvolved parenting style combines being undemanding with indifferent, rejecting behaviour. Uninvolved parents show little commitment to caregiving beyond the minimum effort required to feed and clothe the child. Often this parent is emotionally detached and generally has little time and energy for their child. As a result, they may respond to the child's demands for easily accessible objects, but any efforts that involve long-term goals, such as establishing and enforcing rules about homework and acceptable behaviour, are weak and fleeting.

At the extreme, uninvolved parenting can become neglectful of the child's needs. For example, a single mother of a girl aged nine would spend most evenings at the local slot machine club until she lost all of her money or until the club closed. The mother would leave the girl at home alone and all too often wouldn't get back home until as late as 3 a.m. Frequently the daughter would have to fend for herself and prepare her own evening meals, usually a can of baked beans on toast.

Despite living in a suburb where it was considered unsafe for adults to walk alone at night, on many occasions the girl walked to the slot machine club at night looking for her mother, to get money to buy food for her evening meal. As she was a minor she would have to sit and wait in the restaurant area until a security guard fetched her mother. Often the girl would be left alone for extended periods of time while waiting, and would then walk back home. A few times the girl insisted that her mother walk her home, as she felt too frightened to walk home alone in the dark, but the girl learned very quickly that this would only make her mother angry.

There is a connection between parental support and involvement and a child's antisocial behaviour. A lack of parental support and involvement in their child's life, as found in the uninvolved parenting style, is related to increasing aggression and delinquent behaviour in children, particularly in adolescent boys, who are at a heightened risk of engaging in serious and long-term offending behaviour.

The uninvolved parent is described as:

- Being uninvolved in their child's life and child rearing responsibilities.
- Undemanding, rejecting, indifferent.
- Having little commitment to caregiving (may only do the absolute necessary caregiving such as feeding and clothing the child).
- Being emotionally detached from the child.
- Showing low levels of both warmth and control.
- Having little time or energy for the child.
- Enforcing rules and demands that are weak and fleeting (primarily to suit the needs of the parent at the time).
- Failing in their responsibilities to offer their child guidance or leadership.
- Generally being uninterested in their child.
- Almost neglecting their child if the level of uninvolvement is high.

We also know that parents who are uninvolved in their child's lives are prone to depression, tend to have quite a lot of stressors in their lives and have little or no familial and social support. Unfortunately all of these factors disrupt and disturb every part of the child's development, including parent–child attachment, play and their emotional and social skills development. Even if parental uninvolvement is less extreme, it is still related to adjustment problems. For example, children whose parents have little interaction with them show little or no interest in their school life and struggle with life on many different levels.

WHAT ABOUT THE EFFECTS ON THE CHILDREN OF UNINVOLVED PARENTS?

Children raised with uninvolved parents tend to suffer. Here is a list of the things children struggle with in homes where their parents are uninvolved.

- Neglectful parenting is significantly linked with low-achieving students.
- Uninvolved parenting places the child at risk of developing low self-esteem and impaired social control.
- They are very poor at regulating their emotions and are aggressive, with acting out behaviour.
- They tend to struggle at school and can become school dropouts, which leads to an increased risk of frequent drug use and delinquency.

As one fifteen-year-old male reported, 'If my mum just did her job, I wouldn't be so angry. She says she cares but she doesn't. If she really cared she'd spend time with us.'

Take a moment to ask yourself the following questions.

1. Does it appear this parenting style would be very effective? Why or why not?
2. How do think this parenting style might impact the child?
3. Why would a child parented in this way tend to show more anger and aggression?
4. What do you think might be the immediate and long-term social and emotional consequences for this child (for example, interpersonal difficulties, relationship difficulties, employment difficulties)?
5. Why do you think that might occur?
6. What are the potential immediate and long-term educational implications for a child living in an uninvolved home?

AUTHORITATIVE PARENTING

While reading through the following section, keep in mind the three different parenting styles you have learned about so far and compare them to the authoritative parenting style.

The authoritative style is considered to be the most balanced, well-adjusted, stable, and unwavering approach to child rearing. This is because the authoritative parenting style is marked by firm rules and shared decision-making in a warm, loving and supportive environment. Authoritative parenting is characterized by acceptance, interactional warmth and responsiveness, unconditional love for the child as an individual, and treating the child with kindness and dignity. Authoritative parenting shows respect towards the whole child – the child's personality, likes, dislikes, temperament, strengths and limitations.

Authoritative parents make reasonable demands of their child based on the child's abilities and maturity. They enforce these demands by setting limits and insisting that the child obey. This is also where the parent expresses warmth and affection, and they listen patiently to their child's point of view, and encourage participation in family decision-making. It is a rational, democratic approach that recognizes and respects the rights of both the parents and children. In general, authoritative parents are described as:

- Having a rational, democratic approach that recognizes and respects the rights of both the parents and children.
- Being warm, responsive and involved in the child's life.
- Showing love to their children and making a point of expressing their affection.
- Praising their children and constantly showing approval.
- Really enjoying their children.
- Being consistent in establishing rules and enforcing guidelines, and setting behavioural limitations. Using a rational and reasonable use of firm control while demanding age-appropriate behaviour.
- Permitting and prompting autonomous behaviour and decision-making.
- Providing structure for their children as well as promoting a healthy autonomy by permitting their children a certain amount of freedom and the opportunity to express their desires and preferences.

- Understanding that respect for the parent is earned and also knowing parental authority is accepted by the children through trust.
- Establishing an emotional connection with the children and permitting the children to express thoughts and feelings.
- Teaching their children how to help themselves and showing them self-control.

As you can see these characteristics are seen as involving the three core dimensions of acceptance, using appropriate behavioural control methods and monitoring their child's whereabouts and activities, and facilitating psychological autonomy. It's not about oppressing children or potentially escalating their aggression by forceful attempts at controlling misbehaviour. It's not about giving in to children who are acting out, and it's clearly not about detaching or being uninvolved in the child's life. Authoritative parenting is believed to be the parenting style most likely to aid the development of self-reliance, healthy self-esteem, and a sense of social responsibility in a child. Remember the first chapter on the Belongingness Hypothesis? This theory made it clear that all children need a secure attachment for healthy psychological development. We know that a warm, responsive and dependable parenting style is key.

There is one point from the description above that often needs clarification with parents who come to see me at my clinic. The authoritative parent's ability to actively encourage decision-making is vastly different to the hallmark feature of the permissive parent who allows their children to make their own decisions without parental advice or guidance. The authoritative parent involves the child in age-appropriate decision-making and will encourage their efforts, support them, help them, guide them and instruct them. This parent will also say NO when the occasion calls for it. In this instance the child's decision does not take precedence over the family's decision nor does the child have the power over the parents or the family. The authoritative parent will encourage the children to be a part of family decision-making but responsibility for the final decision will ultimately fall to the parent.

Take a moment to ask yourself the following questions.

1. Does it appear this parenting style would be very effective? Why or why not?
2. How do think this parenting style might impact the child?
3. What do you think might be the immediate and long-term social, emotional and psychological consequences for this child (for example, interpersonal benefits, relationship benefits, employment benefits)?
4. Why do you think that might occur?
5. What are the potential immediate and long-term educational implications for a child living in an authoritative home?

WHAT MAKES THE AUTHORITATIVE PARENTING STYLE SO EFFECTIVE?

- The child will more likely comply with control that appears fair and reasonable rather than arbitrary. Rather than yell and scream insults at their child (for example,

'You stupid boy, can't you do anything I tell you?'), this parent will explain to their child the reasons for the consequences and use privileges as discipline.

- The authoritative parent is nurturing and secure in the standards they set for their children. They effectively model to their children caring concern and confident, self-controlled behaviour. Perhaps for this reason, children of the authoritative parent are advanced in emotional self-regulation and emotional and social understanding. These factors are linked to social competence with peers.
- Parents who combine warmth with rational and reasonable control are likely to be more effective at reinforcing limitations for their child's behaviour. They will more likely praise their children for striving to meet their expectations and make good use of disapproval, which works best when applied by an adult who has been warm and caring.
- Authoritative parents make demands that fit with their children's ability to take responsibility for their own behaviour. As a result these parents let children know they are competent individuals who can do things successfully for themselves, thereby fostering high self-esteem and cognitive and social maturity.
- Supportive aspects of the authoritative style, including parental warmth, involvement and discussion, help protect children from the negative effects of family stress.

WHAT ABOUT THE EFFECTS ON THE CHILDREN OF AUTHORITATIVE PARENTS?

Children from authoritative homes develop especially well because:

- They are self-confident in their mastery of new skills.
- They are self-controlled in their ability to resist engaging in disruptive behaviour (read ahead for more on self-control).
- Authoritative parenting has also been linked to social and moral maturity, involvement in school learning, and academic achievement in high school in older children. (Read ahead for more on academic achievement.)
- They experience less psychological distress, fewer problem behaviours and better peer relations.
- They have higher levels of competence, autonomy and self-reliance. (Read ahead for more on competence.)
- These children also appear to be more emotionally secure.
- Having encountered constant empathy they are less likely to be explosive, and are more likely to show empathy to others. Empathy, is considered to be a core social and emotional competency. Learning core competencies such as empathy reduces aggressive behaviour in children and adolescents.
- Authoritative parenting reduces the risk of affiliation with irresponsible or antisocial peers and involvement in delinquent behaviour, which means fewer conduct problems.
- They tend to develop friendships with well-adjusted peers.
- They are lively and happy in mood.

Children with authoritative parents, who are warm and accepting and set reasonable age-appropriate expectations for behaviour, tend to really feel quite good about themselves. This is because this type of parenting sends a powerful message to the children that they are accepted as competent and worthwhile. This type of parent sets reasonable behavioural expectations and provides suitable explanations for those expectations, helps their child develop the skill of sensible decision-making and helps them learn how to evaluate their own behaviour across a range of circumstances and situations. Having such a close and loving relationship with their parents is one of the most important foundations upon which children literally determine whether or not they are adequate.

Coming from a family practising this parenting style leads to a development of competency in children, as a direct result of their parents believing in them. The parents believe their children have good qualities, they value their children, and like them for who they are. Competent children tend to have a strong parent–child relationship with few arguments and little conflict. It is amazing to see that when children have good relationships with their parents they tend to have a healthy self-concept, believe they have worth, tend to have good relationships all around, perform quite well academically and have stable employment. Such homes are the foundation where children learn to develop how to have lasting and meaningful relationships throughout their lives.

It has been shown, too, that children who have these close, loving and supportive relationships with their parents also do very well academically. Time and again they score higher on intelligence tests and exams, are generally well liked by their peers, and are far better at controlling their emotions than children who don't have such relationships with their parents.

DIFFERENT PARENTING STYLES HOMEWORK

You have just finished reading a lot of information about four very different parenting styles (Authoritarian, Permissive, Uninvolved and Authoritative). Following is an opportunity for you to begin cementing the material from this chapter into your memory. Take the opportunity as parents to discuss this information together and then work through the questions set out below. You will need to consider each question carefully before answering.

1. Of the four different parenting styles (Authoritarian, Permissive, Uninvolved, and Authoritative) which style would describe you best?
2. Why do you practise this style of parenting?
3. Do you think this style of parenting has been successful for you? Provide some reasons for your answer.
4. Make a list of the desires, dreams and goals you have for your family. For instance, what sort of relationship do you want with your children in five years? What goals do you have for your family? What do you want your family to achieve? Then list how you propose to reach those goals, dreams and desires.

After reading this chapter you should be well aware of your parenting style and whether it is effective or not. The next chapters are all about teaching you how to be an authoritative parent, and the best place to start is learning how to effectively communicate with your child at any age.

THREE

Active and Reflective Listening

The most important thing in communication is hearing what isn't being said. The art of reading between the lines is a lifelong quest of the wise. – Shannon L. Alder

This chapter primarily focuses on teaching basic communication skills and takes advantage of active and reflective listening as two primary communication styles. Active listening is simply viewing word use, emotional expression and behaviours as cues from your child in order to open up communication. Reflective listening makes use of a number of listening skills, including reflecting meaning (for example, 'So what I think you're telling me is…'), reflecting feelings (for example, 'You look upset, sounds like you're angry', 'I guess you're feeling…'), paraphrasing (for example, a concise response stating the essence of the other's content in the listener's own words), and empathy (for example, 'I can understand how that must make you feel' or 'That must have been [insert emotive word here] for you').

You can learn how to better parent your child if you are willing to listen to them. Obviously this is not the same as the permissive parenting style where the parent allows the child to 'rule' their own life. A listening parent is being sensitive to their child's unique needs and being willing to permit their child to express those needs without reprisal. However, this does not translate to meeting every 'need' your child believes he has. For example, it seems every child has a need for candy or a new toy or a new electronic game or the latest iPhone each time they go to the supermarket with you. Not every one of your child's needs is beneficial.

This chapter presents common, yet highly effective, communication skills that will help you to develop a far more effective means of talking with your child. It may surprise some parents to learn that their children experience the same joys, fears, anxieties and concerns as they do. This is an opportunity for you to really begin developing a relationship with your child. As one professor stated, '*Children need to know that they are liked, that you are interested in their thoughts, ideas and opinions, their appearance and their beliefs.'* (Robinson, 2013)

Well-known American psychologist, researcher and marriage counsellor John Gottman found in one of his studies on marriage that he was able to predict with 93.6 per cent accuracy whether a marriage would succeed or fail. According to Gottman there are revealing 'signs' of a failing relationship including the Harsh Start-up (for example, when a discussion leads off with criticism and/or sarcasm).

Gottman suggested couples' relationships are doomed to fail not as a result of how often they argue or what they argue about, but rather *how* they argue. Relationships where couples communicate negativity towards each other, such as making accusations or directing blame toward their partner, are doomed to fail. Gottman further explored the lethal nature of the 'Four Horsemen of the Apocalypse'. They are criticism, contempt, defensiveness, and stonewalling. Criticism focuses on blaming and usually involves character assassination by focusing on the individual's personality (for example, 'You're so lazy'). While Gottman's theory is applied to marriages and is used for marital counselling, clinicians often see this very type of negativity with parents interacting with their children. We hear parents' attempts to disguise their critical remarks directed to or about their children with comments like, 'He's just being lazy' or 'She's just being naughty'. Then the parents attempt to justify this negativity with comments like, 'It's just constructive criticism' or 'He knows what I mean', when it is little more than negative criticism directed at the child's character. Contempt, the second of the Four Horsemen, is described as cynicism, name-calling, eye rolling, sneering, mockery and hostile humour. Gottman found contempt to be the worst of the Four Horsemen, and the most poisonous to relationships, as it sends a message of disgust to the spouse, partner or child. Children as young as four can correctly identify the emotion in about half of the faces they see. If this is the communication style practised between parent and child, is there any wonder the parent–child relationship is damaged?

Over the years I have come to recognize that one of the frustrations parents often report is a lack of understanding or a complete misunderstanding of exactly what it is their child is trying to tell them. Given the developmental limitations of children of all ages, parents' attempts at communicating their ideas or demands clearly may be misunderstood by their child. This can lead parents to believe that their child is actively disobeying their requests or ignoring them. One angry mother clearly demonstrated this when she stated, 'He knows better than that. I have told him so many times, he's just being disobedient.' Equally, the parent may not understand just what it is their child is trying to tell them. Developmental limitations certainly play a major role in both the younger child and early adolescent's ability to effectively and clearly communicate thoughts and feelings. When the parent becomes frustrated or ridicules, criticizes, punishes or suppresses their child's attempt to talk about their thoughts and feelings, the child will be less likely to try talking about their thoughts and feelings a second time. Unfortunately, when such exchanges take place it can severely limit the parent–child relationship from developing into a deeper and more meaningful relationship.

Professionals all over the world who work with children are keenly aware that particular developmental limitations children experience can frustrate them to a point where they can have many explosive episodes. These explosive episodes can occur as a result of limitations in language processing skills that leave the child finding it very difficult to verbalize their frustrations and understand complicated demands. When a parent misunderstands a child's needs or the need is poorly specified, the problems remain unresolved and this can be expressed through the child's behaviour. In terms of active listening, one mother told me that with her four-year-old son, 'I cannot believe how easy it is to use and how effective it is with my son. If I practise active listening with him he calms down almost straightaway.' Given this example, there needs to be an understanding that parents are charged with the responsibility of patiently teaching their child to effectively express their thoughts and feelings. This provides you with the opportunity to expand your child's emotional knowledge and development and in so doing further expands the child's developing vocabulary range. This process also helps your child to label and articulate their emotional states.

In many cultures it is often considered rude and inappropriate for a listener to fail their responsibilities of adhering to the 'social rules' of communication. Interestingly, when asked how they would feel if I were to turn away from them and begin a game on my computer or begin to read a book rather than paying attention to them, most parents sitting in my office tell me this is an obvious lack of respect for them, or at the very least that I am simply not interested in helping them. Yet, when it comes to adult–child communication, the rules often change. For instance, parents can show frustration towards the child for not 'getting to the point' quickly enough or failing to make eye contact or failing to show they are really interested in what the child is communicating by use of both verbal and non-verbal communication cues. It is a well-known fact that a child is less likely to act out when they are receiving adequate attention and when the child is accustomed to be being listened to. If we are to agree and recognize that children feel emotional pain in the same way as adults, we must also recognize that the way adults communicate to children has the same impact on the parent–child relationship as it does on adult relationships.

Think back to the time when you and your spouse were dating. Most couples tend to spend a great deal of time together just getting to know each other. Of all the things you did together, perhaps the most important of them all was just talking with each other. Through this you became aware of each other's values, morals and beliefs. You became aware of what was important to your partner and as time went on you began to discuss issues that you might have been struggling with. You began to turn to each other for emotional support, you sought comfort from each other. You developed a trust and your relationship grew as time went on. You became aware of offensive behaviours or those behaviours appreciated by your partner, and no doubt you were aware that if you wanted to maintain a close and respectful relationship you adjusted your behaviours as necessary. Suppose for a moment each time you went out on a date, your partner hardly spoke a word for the entire evening? Or suppose your partner's only communication was to instruct you to do something for them? If this was to happen, ask yourself the following questions:

1. How far do you think your relationship might have developed if you had not spent time just talking with each other?
2. How would you have responded if, on a date, your partner just provided instructions to you, or kept making demands of you?
3. How would you feel if your partner kept getting angry because you were interrupting with 'silly' questions when they were trying to watch the news on television?
4. Do you think you would have continued to invest time and energy trying to develop a meaningful relationship?
5. Do you think you would have decided to marry such a person?

The same principle applies to your children. If you really want to get to know your children and have a close and meaningful relationship with them, you must invest that same time and energy in developing open and honest communication. This is the cornerstone of any relationship.

Children of all ages are very much aware of global events, as media outlets and schools inform them; they will also overhear you discussing these issues. But many parents fail to realize their children have their own thoughts, feelings, values and ideas about such issues. In order to connect emotionally, really connect, you need to spend time with your children discussing thoughts, feelings and ideas with them. The basis of any lasting relationship is open, non-judgmental communication.

HOW WELL DO YOU COMMUNICATE WITH YOUR CHILD?

Parents typically believe they really know and understand their child and have frequently told me they have an intimate knowledge of their child's world. However, when put to the test, they soon realize their knowledge of their child's world isn't as thorough as they once believed. Try answering the questions below. The only rule when answering these questions is to refrain from providing a general answer. You need to provide as much detail as you can.

- Provide details of your child's thoughts, feelings and beliefs about friendships and/or relationships. For example, are you aware of your child's thoughts and beliefs about dating or friendships? What qualities is your child seeking in a partner or friend?

- What are your child's thoughts, feelings and beliefs about current world issues? For instance, the war on terrorism has been in operation for a number of years now. Many allied men and women have lost their lives and received life-threatening injuries. Yet the war continues. Do you really know your child's thoughts and feelings about the war on terror? Do they completely understand the reasons for the war? Or where it all started? Do they believe they are in harm's way?
- Do they even believe in the war?
- Recently we have seen terrorist attacks in countries across the world. Do your children fear a terrorist attack in their own country or hometown?
- Further, you may enquire of other events such as global warming. For instance, do you know what your child thinks of the global warming issue? Does your child have specific concerns? Do they have any ideas on how to save the planet? There are groups of individuals and scientists who debate the extent of damage global warming is said to have caused. Does your child believe this or do they have their own opinions?
- What are your child's hopes and dreams for the future?
- What are your child's morals, values and life beliefs? Don't just take it for granted that your child has the same beliefs as you and will automatically have the same values and morals. You might be surprised, even shocked, to learn this is often not the case
- Too hard? Well, try this. Name up to five of your child's closest friends. Now name those children's parents!

PREPARING FOR *REALLY* LISTENING

With the developmental difficulties children of all ages experience in communicating their thoughts and feelings, reflective listening is an important tool in the communication repertoire to be used to clarify what it is your child is trying to tell you. This section will focus on reflecting feeling and reflecting content. When you are actively listening to your child, pick up on the cues children commonly use. Tuning in to what your child is saying can be made easier when you differentiate between your child's thoughts and feelings.

Many parents say, 'We're busy and we don't have all the time in the world to stop and talk whenever our kids feel like it'. You're right. Life is busy and seems to get busier every year, but do you tell your spouse you don't want to listen to the drivel that comes out of their mouth? Do you tell your work colleagues or boss you don't have time to talk to them? Do you tell your friends you don't have time to talk to them each time they phone you or come around to see you? As one fourteen-year-old girl told me, 'My mother doesn't have time for me. When she comes home from work all she ever does is call her best friend and talks to her'. I would hazard a guess that if you did treat people this way, you could be sitting in your living room right now wondering why you don't have any friends, confused about why you have an unhappy relationship or angry at your boss for sacking you today!

If you are unable to offer your attention to your child, rather than risk shutting them down you can reinforce your interest in listening to them by nominating a later time to sit and talk. Now be warned that there are problems that can develop from this if you don't follow through with your promise. Equally important is the rule of not too many questions all at once as this may be misinterpreted as interrogation – particularly with an adolescent. One mother reported that up until recently she and her seventeen-year-old daughter rarely sat and talked. After arriving home from school each day the daughter would walk straight through the lounge and spend the rest of the afternoon in her bedroom. After working with me, the mother reported that one afternoon as her daughter arrived home she called out to her and told her she had just made both of them a coffee. Her daughter seemed to appreciate this gesture and came and sat with her mother. The conversation started off slowly as the mother tried to put into practice all the active and reflective skills she could remember. The mother noticed that the more questions she asked her daughter the less willing she was to continue the conversation. Eventually the mother stopped and asked her daughter what was wrong. The answer was, 'You're freaking me out with all these questions.' Effective, open communication takes a lot of hard work and a lot of practice.

A FEW COMMUNICATION 'RULES'

- Get down on the child's level. The very size difference between adult and child carries an undertone of power imbalance in favour of the parent. The issue is about meeting the child of any age at their level, sending a message of validation and equality to the child.
- Make eye contact. It tells your child you are interested in what they have to say. It is not uncommon for parents to continue a task, or read the daily newspaper, or continue

watching the television while their child is attempting to talk with them. What message does this send?

- Take turns. Taking turns in communication is vital if your child is to comfortably express their thoughts and feelings. Some of the most common complaints I hear from children about communicating with their parents have been 'They don't listen to me' and 'When I try to say something, they just cut me off or talk over me.'
- Listen to what is being said rather than thinking about what you are going to say once your child has finished.
- It's unfortunate, but it seems parents rarely discuss their own emotions with their children. It is important to discuss your own feelings and thoughts with your children at an age-appropriate level. However, you must be careful not to be judgmental or blame your child for your negative feeling states. Finally, you must never use your child as a counsellor or use them as a dumping ground for your emotions.
- Use 'I' statements. Generally 'you' statements tend to be delivered as an accusation (for example, 'You never...') or an attack on the listener's personality (for example, 'You're so lazy'). This can cause the listener to become defensive. The defensive listener, feeling blamed, 'fires' back at the speaker and conflict is almost inevitable. By using 'I' statements parents can inform their children how their behaviour impacts them without accusing or blaming the child. 'I' statements also put you in a better position to avoid typically escalating the situation to conflict, and

avoid the hurtful exchanges that all too often accompany arguments (for example, 'I am feeling quite angry at you because we agreed you would do the dishes tonight and they have not been done').

- If children act out what they are feeling, then negative emotional and behavioural expressions *could* be treated as a cue that your child is trying to tell you something. In such instances it can be very helpful to remember two things. 1) ALWAYS ask yourself 'What is my child trying to tell me?' and 2) Without being an interrogator, take on the investigator role with your child, seeking confirmation of what you think your child is trying to tell you. Active and reflective listening is concerned with ensuring the listener really understands the message the speaker is conveying.
- Ask clarifying questions. At this point you will need to understand how to ask your child appropriate questions. To begin with, 'why' questions are something to be avoided if at all possible. 'Why' questions are very difficult to answer, even for adults. Why questions have the connotation of demanding justification for one's actions, attitudes or behaviour, rather than making a genuine inquiry. For instance, when a parent asks the child 'Why did you do that?' it sounds as though the parent is demanding the child justify their behaviour. This unfortunately can result in the child becoming defensive, or overly concerned they might be in trouble with the parent, and can quickly shut down communication.

Furthermore, the listener can react defensively when presented with 'why' questions. Here's an example of how this principle works. Imagine you were 15 minutes late meeting a friend at a café. As you arrived your friend demanded of you 'Why are you late?' How might you react? How might you respond to this questioning? Feeling a little defensive, most people typically begin justifying their behaviour by trying to provide an explanation. As you can see with such a simple example, why questions tend to encourage a defensive response rather than promote open and honest communication.

- 'How come', 'who', 'what', 'when', and 'where' are more appropriate questions to ask when gaining information from your child. This approach further permits open communication and understanding, as your child may not feel as though they have to justify their actions or defend themself.

ACTIVE LISTENING

Active listening is viewing word use, emotional expressions and behaviours as a cue from your child that they want to talk to you or that there may be an issue your child is struggling with but is unable to communicate to you clearly. However, active listening goes well beyond this and also uses basic communication skills. Generally the listener uses minimal phrases, such as 'ah-ha', 'mm-hm', 'yes', 'okay', and 'right'. Further, the listener faces the speaker, makes eye contact, nods in an affirmative manner, and asks appropriate questions to clarify a point or to invite the speaker to provide more information. Again the listener would also ask openended questions that make use of 'what', 'where', 'whom' or 'how'. These responses indicate the listener is there with the speaker, and encourage the speaker to continue telling their story. This principle is no different for children. You can encourage your child to continue their conversation by using these types of basic communication skills. Basic active listening techniques can really help your child tell you their story and identify troubling issues. Active listening skills let your child know you the parent are willing to enter their world, respect their point of view and are really listening to them.

Active listening is more than just a nod of the head; it is listening for cues as to what your child is trying to tell you. Tone of voice, facial expressions and word use, including feeling words, body language and behaviours, are all cues for you to 'listen' for. Missing these cues may mean you miss very important opportunities to develop a deeper relationship with your child. You may also miss the cognitive, physical, spiritual or emotional needs of your child, and further miss the opportunity to aid in their emotional development.

Here's an example of how active listening might work. The most common one-word response a child will provide a parent who asks about their day at school is 'all right, 'good', 'okay', 'eh' or 'bad'. Depending on how your child responded (for example, happy, sad, indifferent) you would take advantage of active listening skills and ask 'What was good about your day?' or 'Can you tell me some things that were good about your day?' or 'It doesn't sound like you had a good day, what happened?' Missing those emotional, facial and behavioural cues can result in missed opportunities to really learn what is happening in your child's world. For example, after completing this session, one mother told me she tried active and reflective listening with her ten-year-old son with worrying results. As usual, she picked him up at the end of the school day and while travelling home she asked him about his day. Her son provided the usual uninterested answer of 'Okay'. But this time the mother persisted and asked her son 'What was okay about your day?' He simply answered 'Nothing.' But this time the mother was aware of the emotional tone of his voice, she saw he was not making eye contact and she saw his shoulders drop. The mother said, 'It doesn't look like nothing happened. It looks like you are upset about something.' Her son burst into tears, telling her that he was being bullied at school every day by a group of boys. Apparently the boys would throw things at him, call him names, push him and hit him. Before that day, before learning how to communicate with her son, this mother never knew what was happening to him. A few simple questions opened up his world and, armed with this information, his mother approached the school and had the bullying stopped.

Timing is also of the essence. Sometimes children are unaccustomed to parents wanting to sit down and have a chat with them. In which case you need to revert back to active listening and wait for a more appropriate moment later in the day or evening to revisit the issue. Further, when conflict does arise or if you or your child is feeling overwhelmed, in the interest of protecting the parent–child relationship, it is recommended the conversation be postponed until such time as both the parent and child are emotionally prepared to discuss the issue calmly. That is, when one party is beginning to feel overwhelmed, they would inform the other member they are taking 15 minutes out. This permits both parties the opportunity to calm down and avoid potential conflict or an ensuing power struggle. If age or maturity is an issue, the responsibility of initiating 'time out' will be the parent's. In this instance, you can simply tell your child that you will discuss the issue of concern at a more appropriate time rather than allowing conflict to take over.

Sometimes parents choose not to say what needs to be said because of the reaction of their child. For example, one mother reported that 'I get so angry and we end up arguing. She goes off into her room, slams the door and stays there.' Until the mother completed this session, the situation between the two was never discussed and the parent–child relationship was beginning to suffer. When discussing the 15-minute rule as a more effective way of avoiding the conflict, the mother suggested, 'Yeah, but if I just walk away she will think she's won'. Apart from the obvious power struggle here it was helpful to inform the mother that the 15-minute rule did not mean she could not raise her concerns. The mother was instructed that when conflict arose she should inform her daughter that she was taking 15 minutes out to calm down, but that they would continue their conversation at a more appropriate time.

Many households in our society are pressed for time. There are employment commitments, after-school sports, evening meals to prepare, house cleaning, dishes to wash, helping children with homework … the list goes on. When discussing effective communication with their children, parents do feel the time constraints in their lives. But there can be some simple ways around these time constraints. For instance, you could discuss your child's day at school (or university or work) while driving home, or to and from their sporting activities, or around the dinner table during the evening meal. It is highly recommended that families sit down together at the dining table for their evening meal. This is often the time when they can all share about their day and a time when the family can really connect.

REFLECTIVE LISTENING

Reflective listening tells your child that you are really listening and doing everything you can to make sure you really understand what you have heard. Reflective listening, then, is the listener's way of checking in with the speaker that the listener truly understands what has been said. This is a very important part of communication as at this point misunderstandings can be commonplace. Reflective listening also allows the speaker an opportunity to correct any misunderstandings or incorrect interpretations they might have *before* an argument can take place.

Reflective listening makes use of a number of listening skills including reflecting meaning, (for example, 'So what I think you're telling me is…'), reflecting feelings (for example, 'You look upset, sounds like you're angry, I guess you're feeling…'), paraphrasing (for example, a concise response stating the essence of the other's content in the listener's own words), and empathy (for example, 'I can understand how that must make you feel' or 'That must have been [insert emotive word here] for you').

Children frequently avoid strong negative emotions as they can be unsure of the feeling they are experiencing, it can be frightening to them and often they don't know how to contain the feeling. A parent who uses 'feeling' words and phrases helps their child get in touch with their feelings, to understand those feelings, to 'know' those feelings, and finally to process those feelings. This is the early stage of developing emotional maturity. The skill base of reflective listening tends to naturally follow active listening. Reflective listening further aids the development of a child's emotional intelligence. Following are a few examples of how reflective listening might work.

- In an attempt to understand the meaning behind the story your child has been telling you, you might try: 'So what I think you're telling me is…'; however, if you have misunderstood what your child is trying to tell you, then you can simply respond with 'I don't quite understand what you're saying. Can you tell me again, maybe in a different way?' or 'I don't get it, tell me again'. This gives you the opportunity to clarify with your child what they are trying to tell you. This obviously assists in effective communication, it permits your child to feel the situation is safe enough to try and tell you again and provides a further sense of validation, and prevents you from assuming what you think your child is saying. If you misunderstand the content, taking this approach will allow your child to clarify the content and thus provide an opportunity to continue the conversation.
- Reflecting feelings requires you to be taking notice of your child's behaviours, the particular word use and the emotion applied to those words. When you are tuned into your child, you are given an opportunity to explore your child's world in greater depth.
- Children will attempt to use feeling words to describe their day or an event or something that is meaningful to them. This will provide you with the opportunity to really

explore with your child the nature of the event and the associated feelings.

- Reflecting feelings also involves you making use of statements that will include feeling words. Further, in collaboration with your child, you are in a position to try and label the apparent emotion your child is presenting. For example, 'You look upset/sad/disappointed' or 'It sounds like you're frustrated/annoyed/angry' or 'You sound happy/excited'. Choose age-appropriate feeling words. For instance, younger children may not necessarily know what 'frustrated' or 'annoyed' means, but they may have a pretty good idea of what 'mad' means.
- Paraphrasing. This is a concise response stating the essence of what the other person has been saying in your own words. By paraphrasing you are attempting to repeat back to your child the most important details of what they have said in both their own words and in a clearer way. This really sends the message to your child that you have heard them and are trying to understand them and engage with them.
- Repeating back verbatim can be an arduous task, so it's best to keep it to 'short' replies. It is an effective tool to use as it simply makes it very clear to your child that you are with them in the conversation. For instance, the underlying message sent to your child is, 'I hear you', 'I'm interested in what you are saying' and so on. Thus promoting further conversation between the two of you.
- Empathy. We all like someone to empathize with us at times, especially when we have had a particularly difficult

time. Gaining empathy from someone we love seems to have a healing effect in our lives. We feel supported by our loved one and gain strength to continue in that difficult circumstance. When someone shows us empathy we are able to process those intense negative feelings and feel as if the situation may not be as overwhelming as we previously thought. An empathic parent can also help to make their child feel safe. Empathy is a vital component of effective communication as it also demonstrates that you are able to sympathize with your child.

MORE PHRASES THAT CAN OPEN UP AND KEEP A CONVERSATION MOVING

- 'I want to know what you have to say about it.'
- 'Is there anything more you want to talk to me about?'
- 'What do you think about...?'
- 'Would you like to talk to me about…?'
- 'Can you explain that to me?'
- 'Can you explain that again differently?'
- 'How do you feel about that?'
- 'Do you mean…?'
- 'Do you feel [for example, mad, bad, happy or sad]?'

DEVELOPMENTAL DIFFERENCES

The age or the developmental maturity of your child will guide the type of conversation you will have and determine the kind of questions you might ask your child. The younger child will understand simple, emotive words such as mad, bad, glad and sad. The middle-age child will have a greater emotional understanding and vocabulary, while the adolescent will be further advanced. As such you have an opportunity to insert emotive words in reflective listening. For example, 'It sounds like you are frustrated about…', or 'You look disappointed about…', or 'It sounds like you are very excited about…'. Any combination of reflective listening responses can be used provided you insert an emotive term. This also adds to your child's emotional vocabulary repertoire. While the older child/adolescent is developmentally more capable of labelling feelings and verbalizing those feelings, you can still aid their developing emotional intelligence by asking about their thoughts on the matter at hand. For example, 'What are your thoughts about that?' or 'What are you thinking about?' or 'How do feel about that?'. This approach opens up an opportunity for the older child/adolescent to verbalize both their feelings and their thoughts.

Sometimes a child will tell their parent a long drawn-out story of an event with seemingly unimportant and unrelated facts (as I mention this to parents, I watch for their responses such as rolling their eyes, or even comments such as 'Yeah, the drivel he comes out with!'). You really do need to understand that you must remain patient and allow your child to tell you their story, as this is the time they are trying to reach out to you. Remember, if your child is met with a negative response when they are trying to talk about their feelings, they are less likely to attempt this a second time. This is an opportunity for you to practise the skills of communication and to show your child you are interested in their story and thus interested in them.

ACTIVE AND REFLECTIVE LISTENING SKILLS HOMEWORK

This chapter was about the importance of really listening to your child and outlined two of the most effective communication skills – active and reflective listening. You have read about the various cues your child might use (emotionally laden words, tone of voice and behaviour) in an attempt to communicate their thoughts and feelings to you. You have also learned about the importance of *not* assuming you automatically know what it is your child is trying to tell you. Finally, you also read about reflecting back both your understanding of what you think your child is trying to tell you, and reflecting back their feelings.

Remember to be aware of the clues and ask yourself 'What is my child trying to tell me?'

1. Practise active listening with your child at least twice this week.
2. Practise reflective listening with your child at least twice this week.
3. Practise active listening with your spouse at least twice this week.
4. Practise reflective listening with your spouse at least twice this week.
5. How well do you rate your effort and the results?
6. Did you notice any changes in the way you communicated with both your child and your spouse?
7. Have you noticed any changes in your relationships with your child and/or your spouse?

FOUR

Emotional and Behavioural Involvement

Your children need your presence more than your presents.
– Jesse Jackson

Children need to connect emotionally with their parents. Developing an emotional attachment with your child means sharing an interest in their life, in their thoughts and feelings, in their joys and disappointments, in their likes and dislikes and in their successes and failures. It also means using words of comfort and understanding, using words of support, sharing understanding, and using physical touch with your child such as cuddling. Emotional and behavioural involvement is saying to your child 'I love you' in a way your child understands. Emotional and behavioural involvement is all about you spending quality time with your child and taking the time to build both a friendship and an emotional connection with them, while forever remaining the authoritative parent. You may remember that the authoritative parent is warm, loving and accepting, yet sets firm boundaries for the child.

GETTING INVOLVED

Before you go ahead and read this chapter, take a few moments to think about the time before you became a parent, when it was just you and your spouse or partner. Think about when you were dating and all the things you did together just so you could spend quality time with each other, and then answer the following questions.

1. When you were dating what would you do to spend time together?
2. Where would you go?
3. How often would you go out together?
4. When you weren't together, how often would you talk to each other during the week? That includes using all forms of social media to make contact with each other.
5. What things did you talk about?
6. At what point did you discuss with each other your values, your morals, your beliefs, your disappointments and hurts and the joys you had experienced, your goals and dreams and hopes in life?

Based on your answers to the above questions, you would have recognized just how important it was for your relationship that you spent time together. You invested quality time into developing and building your relationship. You understood the importance of investing time into developing an emotional connection;

without this continued investment of time you would not have developed a strong foundation for a stable or mature relationship. This principle of spending quality time together and making an emotional connection is no different for you and your child.

Consider the following questions:

1. Think back to when you were dating. How far do you think your relationship would have developed if you had not spent quality time together?
2. Supposing each time you went out on a date you hardly spoke a word to each other. Do you think your relationship would have gone very far?
3. Or suppose that when on a date the only time your partner spoke to you was to tell you to do something for them. Would you have wanted to continue that relationship?
4. How far do you think your relationship would have developed if your partner showed no concern for your interests?

As an adult you might try to raise your concerns with your spouse or partner, or you may choose to leave the relationship if you feel it is not moving forward or is no longer working. That's okay for an adult, but what about a child? Children typically can't just walk out on their parents. They don't always have the developmental maturity to discuss their concerns with you, and if they did, they still have to risk you rejecting them and their efforts while trying to tell what is troubling them. Imagine your child saying to you:

'*I'm not happy with the current state of our relationship and I don't appreciate the way you speak to me and spend so little time with me.*

If you don't start treating me with the respect I deserve, I will have no other choice but to re-evaluate where this relationship is going.'

While some parents might need to hear such a comment from their children, it is unlikely it is going to happen. In a sense, like it or not, your child is caught in the parent–child relationship. The principle here is simply that the relationship 'rules' applied to adult relationships often appear to be forgotten or even ignored in the parent–child relationship, yet these relationship rules are vital to the very survival of the parent–child relationship. Emotional involvement means learning about and becoming involved with your child's interests, likes, dislikes, values, morals, convictions, hopes, dreams, aspirations and disappointments and thoughts and feelings. It means spending quality time talking with your child and getting to know who they are. So how do you as parents begin developing an emotional connection with your child?

DEVELOPING AN EMOTIONAL CONNECTION WITH YOUR CHILD

- Children of all ages need an emotional connection with their parents, even teenagers and adults. That emotional connection to parents remains vitally important throughout the course of our life. One of the foundations of developing an emotional connection with your child is sharing in their interests. For instance, your child may like discussing the latest Xbox games or their try-outs for the local football team (or other age-appropriate interests), but it bores you to tears or makes no sense to you at all. You need to share in these interests with your child and become a part of their world. In order to begin building an emotional connection with your child, you must understand that the beginning of a relationship starts with sharing and developing mutual interests with the other person; in this instance it is your child. A helpful way to put this into perspective is to think of examples from your own life.

- An emotional connection is further developed through the art of active and reflective listening as you are taking the time to hear your child's thoughts, ideas and beliefs and then responding appropriately.
- Share in your child's feelings (this will be discussed at length in Chapter 5 on accepting children's feelings and behaviour). Try to understand what they must be feeling and why they might be feeling that way. For example, when they arrive home from school and tell you they have had a fight with a friend, don't dismiss their thoughts and feelings as silly and unimportant. Ask yourself how you would feel if you had lost a close friend to an argument and your spouse just brushed you off and told you to stop being silly. Remember, where a child has experienced such responses or believes it is unsafe to express their thoughts and feelings due to criticism, punishment, put downs and the like, they are less likely to risk sharing their thoughts and feelings with you again.
- Use words of comfort, support and understanding. When your child is trying to talk about their thoughts and feelings, take the time to listen without judgment, without interrupting them, and without talking over the top of them; just listen. As tempting as it may be, this is not the time to take the high moral ground and begin a

lecture of right and wrong. This can be raised at a more appropriate time when both parties are calm and can remain rational. Even though some events that your child is retelling might not seem a big deal to you, don't brush these incidents off with pat remarks or try to smooth over the concern. Listen to what your child is telling you, be an ear and take it all in.

- Appropriate physical touch conveys a powerful message of 'I love you' to your child. When discussing physical touch it goes without saying this is referring to appropriate and non-sexual physical expressions of love and acceptance through touching such as cuddling and holding hands. From birth, human beings convey and receive love and acceptance through physical touch. Physical touch with children can be anything from a kiss on the cheek to cuddling to holding hands, to a gentle stroke on the arm or back, to sitting on the couch pressing together shoulders or knees. Children of all ages need regular touch as this confirms to them they are loved and accepted by their parent.
- Adolescence is a time of transition from childhood to adult. This is also a time when a child's sense of independence from their parents is being exercised more and more. Commonly the older child and the adolescent appear to withdraw or 'pull back' from expressing and receiving physical affection from their parents. This can be a difficult time for some parents to understand as at times this normal pulling-back behaviour might appear as though your child is absolutely rejecting you or your efforts to really connect with them. However, during this transitional period, the child and the adolescent still need

you to show them your love and you need to continue showing age-appropriate physical affection.

- Developing an emotional connection with your adolescent child is still possible. However, it may mean you need to be a little more ingenious at creating an opportunity to accomplish this goal. For example, you could sit close to them while they are watching the television and touch shoulders, or gently rub a knee briefly, offer a gentle stroke on the arm or tickle their back or hair as they sit at the breakfast table. Or when your adolescent child goes to bed you could sit on the side of their bed and just talk for a few minutes.
- Emotional involvement expresses an attitude of unconditional love, acceptance, approval, and forgiveness, and is expressed both verbally and physically. Unconditional love means that you will behave the same with your child when they succeed and when they push you to your uttermost limits. It means you cannot remain angry once you have disciplined (*not* punished) your child. It means you will encourage them even if they fail. It means your enthusiasm will be the same in the face of failures and successes. It means continued love and acceptance regardless of how your child has behaved.
- Emotional involvement is more than just listening and sharing with your child. You need to say to your child often 'I love you', 'I think you're great', 'I'm so lucky to have a child such as you', 'I'm so proud of you'. You can leave little messages of love and encouragement in their lunchbox or on their pillow, or for the older child you can leave little messages in their school diaries or on their

phone. This will be covered in more detail in Chapter 7 on praise, encouragement and recognition.

- Emotional involvement further includes parental transparency. Children very rarely have the privilege of really knowing who their parents are. Often this is because for whatever reason parents appear to keep their children from entering their emotional and cognitive world. Parental transparency is where you can *appropriately* share your thoughts, feelings and ideas with your children. It means you would also *appropriately* express both positive and negative emotions and allow your children to ask about why you are obviously upset without shutting them out with comments such as 'Never you mind'. Children have an uncanny ability to know when you are upset or angry even before you have spoken a single word, or when you are trying to put on a brave face. Why? Children are the world's best behavioural profilers. They know by your body language – by the way you stand, by your facial expression, tone of voice, the way you walk or sit. These all provide your children with clues to the way you are feeling. They may not always know *why* you are feeling that way – but they know *what* you are feeling!
- How does a relationship between two people grow and thrive when one half of the couple is withholding information about themselves? Sharing appropriate feelings with your child helps to strengthen the parent–child relationship. Your child can learn about those issues that are important to you, what you value or hold dear, what your limitations are, what issues might distress you and so on.

- Parental transparency does not mean you should discuss any and all emotions or use your child as an emotional 'dumping ground' or adult substitute. Responsible parenting means taking responsibility for your own emotions and how you express those emotions (and behaviour!) in a timely and age-appropriate manner. Obviously the amount of detail you would disclose is dependent upon the age of your child, their maturity, their understanding and the appropriateness of the subject matter. This also means then that you cannot blame your child for how you feel. Blaming a child for your feelings and calmly expressing how their behaviours affect you are two very different approaches.

BEHAVIOURAL INVOLVEMENT

Behavioural involvement in your children's lives speaks volumes to them and is considered by professionals to be 'one of the love languages' of children. When we watch children in the playground we see an almost immediate connection with their friends and other children through play. In a child's world it seems just 5 minutes of play is all that is needed to call someone your best friend. When parents play with their children it sends a powerful message that their children are loved, valued and wanted in a way they understand. Play seems to rise above race, religion, disappointments and hurts and provides a time where forgiveness and reconnection are established. As one father keenly aware of his eleven-year-old son's needs put it:

'My son and I go running and bike riding together. If we miss just one night he gets very disappointed.'

Recently I saw a man walking through a shopping centre carpark one sunny afternoon. It was obvious he was heading toward the nearest creek; in one hand he held three fishing rods, a fishing net and a fishing tackle box. As he weaved his way around the parked cars making his way clear of the carpark, I noticed the man had a smile on his face as he looked down at his young daughter. It seemed clear this was a very special father–daughter time and Dad was very excited. At its simplest, behavioural involvement is spending quality time with your children. But it also means taking an interest in the things your child likes and being actively involved in those interests. It means taking the opportunity to spend time on a regular basis being actively involved with your child by doing things together, such as having a regular playtime.

It must be also be noted that parents of adolescent children can also develop both an emotional and behavioural connection with their child by using the principles presented below. The fundamental principle is seeking opportunities to share in your adolescent's interests and to develop and share common interests. This will require constant effort on your part, but it can be achieved. For some parents, spending regular quality time with their child might be somewhat of a foreign concept. But remember the efforts you had to put in to developing your relationship when you were dating. It didn't happen overnight; you had to work at it one step at a time. If spending quality time with your children is new to you, let me encourage you to read this chapter, put the book down, and then try the principles and strategies one step at a time. Learn to invest your time and energy in the important areas of your child's life. Parents investing time – *quality* time – in their children report this is a major key to altering 'misbehaviour'.

What is one of the universal love languages of all children across the world? Play! Play is a universal love language for children. Play can heal a thousand hurts, build instant relationships, reignite fractured and strained friendships and foster closeness with our children. Children crave parental interaction on all levels – especially age-appropriate play. This is such an opportunity to both enjoy the moment and enjoy your children as evidenced by the following statements:

> *'My daughter and I get out all her dolls and teddies and sit down together and have tea parties. She loves it.'*
>
> *'My daughter and I love going kayaking together.'*
>
> *'I put the basketball ring up for my boys; we really enjoy getting out and playing together.'*

Play is quite simply spending quality time with your child and doing things together. One of the saddest and most common problems of modern society is the ever-decreasing family time available to working parents. Without appropriate involvement with your children, how are you to know how to parent your child? How do you know what is important to your child? How do know what your child values or what is important to him or what her life dreams are? How do even know who your child really is? Think of it this way. What if your spouse would only spend a minute a day with you because he/she was so busy with everything else? Would you feel valued by your spouse? You might even begin believing 'other' things are more important to your spouse. Would you consider the relationship was meeting your needs?'

This is one of the things I hear most often when couples come to see me for relationship therapy: 'We just don't talk anymore. We have just grown apart. I guess we just got busy.' This clearly demonstrates that lack of quality time or just lack of time with one's spouse is a major contributor to the demise of the marital relationship. How much more so the parent–child relationship?

Do you remember in Chapter 1 we talked about the Belongingness Hypothesis? The Belongingness Hypothesis makes it really quite clear why play or spending time together is so important. Having contact with people who show no support or are indifferent or uncaring about our needs really doesn't do too much to satisfy that innate need to belong. Knowing that you love them might be emotionally comforting for your children, but it still does not completely meet the need to belong. Simply stated, a child needs a secure attachment with their parents, a safe and secure parent–child relationship and a commitment that goes beyond just caregiving in order for the child's need of belonging to be truly met.

When discussing the issue of spending time with their children, one of the most common responses I hear from parents is, 'I do spend time with him. I take him to his football training each week'. This is missing the point and is not the essence of behavioural involvement. Behavioural involvement in a child's life goes beyond the point of taking your child to their after-school or weekend sporting activities. Behavioural involvement is spending quality time with your children. This means being actively involved in your child's interests and taking the opportunity to regularly play age-appropriate games with them. To really begin understanding just how important it is to be involved in your child's life, think about your own life and your relationships and friendships. Think about how essential spending quality time with those individuals is for the health of your relationships.

Adults tend to recognize the importance of spending time together in various social settings, family gatherings and one-on-one time. Adults tend to understand that quality time is one of the foundations of a strong relationship. Think about playtime in your world and all the fun things you do with your spouse, your friends and family members. This is just a simple exercise to draw your attention to the fact that you not only recognize the importance of spending quality time together to build an understanding of each other's world, but you know this also develops a strong foundation to any of your relationships. This principle is the same for children. How do you expect to play an important part in your child's world if you do not spend quality time together?

Ask yourself how far your relationship would have developed if you were of the opinion your partner didn't want to spend time with you because they were always too tired, or couldn't be bothered, or were always too busy. How would you have felt about this? Would you have felt you weren't good enough because your partner never really wanted to spend quality time with you? Would you have felt angry or disappointed? Children of all ages need to spend quality time with their parents. The key question is how much quality time should be spent with children and how often should you play with your children? Regular, frequent play is the answer, as often as possible. For instance, you could set time aside when arriving home from the after-school pick-up or after the evening meal to play a board game, a card game, rough and tumble play, backyard cricket, or kick the ball at the local community playground or park.

It can be an interesting exercise to watch parents' responses to this as some parents will argue with me that they are simply too busy or too tired to spend time with their children. Or the opposite has happened. Some parents have felt so guilty at the lack of quality time they spend with their children that they go from one extreme of no or little time with their child to the other extreme of wanting to spend hours at a time with their children to make up for the time they've missed out on. Spending quality time with your children is not necessarily achieved by spending hours and hours of time.

I remember one parent who, while working her way through my parenting course, felt so bad, so guilty and even a failure as a mother when she realized she really didn't spend *any* quality time with her children. She was determined that this was going to change. So she went from spending virtually no quality time with her young children to trying to spend hours each afternoon after school with them. In just two weeks the mother was reporting she must have been doing something wrong as her children were complaining about having to stay at the playground. When I asked the mother about this she told me that she was taking her children to the playground for an hour every day after school to play. While in the beginning the children thought this was a whole lot of fun, there were days when they didn't want to or need to be there for the hour. But the mother thought that if the children weren't there for the entire hour she was somehow failing to spend quality time with them. So she made them stay at the park.

Emotionally connecting with your child might simply mean sitting together and just talking, going to a café and having a cuppa, or stopping and having an ice-cream together on the way home from school. The important thing to remember is to make time for your children, to set aside regular time with them, having fun, talking and playing with them. Even once a week is beneficial to the parent–child relationship and weekends are another great opportunity for parent–child activities.

Finally, children can be unaccustomed to spending quality time with parents and particularly having one-on-one time with either of their parents. I highly recommended that same-sex and opposite-sex parent–child 'dates' take place about once a month. This provides the opportunity to develop quality one-on-one time and for parents to really connect with their child. It is a great opportunity for dad to teach his daughter how she should expect to be treated and respected by men and it's an opportunity for sons to learn how to treat and respect women when out on a date with their mothers. Remember, the point of behavioural and emotional involvement is to begin the process of developing a close supportive bond between parent and child. Multiple-child families are also able to manage this if the parents alternate the dates between their children.

RULES FOR PLAY

1. Throughout the week each member of the family has a turn in choosing a game.
2. Don't become competitive with your child.
3. Do allow your child to win and lose.
4. Permit your child to discuss the rules of the game with you. Some games parents played as children are played differently today.
5. Have fun.

SOME BEHAVIOURAL INVOLVEMENT IDEAS

While the list is endless, some ideas include:

- Bike riding
- Exercising together
- Walking together
- Visiting the local playground
- Card games
- Board games
- Nature walks
- Camping
- Fishing
- Bowling
- Backyard cricket
- Basketball
- Netball
- Football
- Tea parties with all the dolls or teddy bears
- Using Lego to create a masterpiece
- Talking around the evening meal
- Developing hobbies together
- Becoming involved in hobbies where the entire family joins in
- Indoor rock-climbing
- Mini golf
- Gym membership
- Clothes shopping
- Rowing

- Skiing
- Scrapbooking
- Having an ice-cream together (or for the older adolescent a hot chocolate or coffee)
- Joining a martial arts club
- Hunting
- Shooting
- Dollhouse play
- Wrestling on the lounge room floor
- Helping with homework
- Go-kart racing

Did you notice there is no reference to technology or screens of any kind? Any electronic item such as the television, computer, PlayStation, Xbox, mobile phone, iPod, iPad, tablets or any handheld game such as a Game Boy is considered a screen. Screens do not contribute to spending quality time together. Why? We know that children and adults typically 'enter' the world of the electronic game; the individual can become so involved in the game that they lose all perspective of time and place. As the individual is generally unaware of their surroundings, gaming becomes very individualistic; there is no communication and no emotional connecting.

Some parents have told me they go home and try setting up regular fun time or play time with their children, but their children are more interested in screen-time and that if their children are not permitted to have this screen-time, they refuse to participate in any games or activities the rest of the family have chosen to play. I encourage you to keep trying. Children will often opt for electronic games – particularly if the child's electronic game play has had little regulation by the parent. The child can sit out on the family game time if they refuse to participate, but they are not permitted to then play electronic games or watch television. While explaining all the research on the dangers and problems of technology and how they are negatively impacting our children is beyond the scope of this book, below is just a short but very concerning list.

TECHNOLOGY AND WHAT IT DOES TO CHILDREN

- Technology has been found to reduce a child's sleep.
- It has been found to reduce a child's social skills or impede the development of social skills.
- Children do not learn the art of give and take.
- They do not learn how to manage difficult situations arising in friendships or relationships and they do not learn how to successfully navigate these situations.
- It is related to childhood obesity.
- It is related to depression developing in children.
- It can contribute to social phobia.
- Excessive gaming can increase aggression in boys.
- Research has found children are actually at risk of developing dependence or an addiction to gaming.

If your children are refusing to engage in games or family time in favour of screens, there are a few things you can do to combat this. First of all, you may need to restrict the amount of time your children spend on screens each day. It is simply not healthy for children to be spending too much time on screens. For instance, as screen-time has been found to negatively influence a child's ability to relax and sleep, under no circumstances should children be allowed to use technology up until their bedtime or in bed for that matter. I recommend parents make sure that *all* chores, homework and other responsibilities are completed *before* the child is allowed to use electronics. I recommend that no child – regardless of age – should spend more than an hour on screens or social media per day. Technology use should be limited with a very clear understanding of start and finish times.

EMOTIONAL AND BEHAVIOURAL HOMEWORK

This chapter discussed how children primarily develop a sense of self based on their interactions and the quality of their relationship with those who are most important in their life.

Developing an emotional attachment with your child can be accomplished by developing shared interests, sharing thoughts, feelings, values and morals on various topics. Developing an emotional attachment is further achieved by using words of comfort, support and understanding. Also, developing an emotional attachment in your child's life requires both verbal and physical expressions of love such as saying 'I love you' or 'You're special to me' and by cuddling, holding hands or giving a tender stroke on the arm. During this chapter you also learned how important it is to be transparent with your child, and to recognize your limitations and be ready to apologize to your child when the need arises. Believe it or not, this is an extremely important component of developing an emotional attachment with your child.

You also learned that people need regular quality time with the ones they love. Children especially need quality time with their parents. By committing to quality time in a child's life you are cementing in their minds how important they are to you. Remember when you were dating; how far would your relationship have gone if your partner was not prepared to spend quality, one-on-one time with you? Think about how special you felt, how good you felt about yourself when this person wanted to spend time with just you.

It is vital for families to spend quality time together as well as one-on-one time with each other. For this chapter your homework is to begin a lifelong process of maintaining regular quality time with your children and family and to organize monthly dates with your children.

- During the following week make at least three attempts at developing an emotional connection with your child.
- During the following week make at least three attempts at spending quality time with your child.
- It is also important to continue practising active and reflective listening skills.

FIVE

Accepting Children's Emotions and Behaviour and Enhancing the Development of Emotional Intelligence in Children

When I was a child, I spoke as a child, I understood as a child, I thought as a child; but when I became a man, I put away childish things. – 1 Corinthians, 13:11, King James' Bible

One afternoon during the school holidays I saw a mother go into an electronics store with her two sons. One son, who was about ten years old, was so excited to see all the different electronic games for sale that he went from shelf to shelf examining all the different games and eagerly reading the description of each game on the back cover. The boy became very excited after finding one particular game. Holding on to it, he ran to his mother who was standing in a line waiting to be served. The boy was desperately trying to gain his mother's attention to show her the wonderful game he had found, calling out to her, 'Look, Mum, look at the game I found!', with unbridled eagerness. The mother turned towards her son, bent down and angrily yelled, 'You're an animal.' This poor little boy's face turned from excitement to disappointment and hurt as he tried to recover from the cruel words his mother had screamed at him.

One of the most common questions I am asked is 'What is normal childhood behaviour?' Believe it or not, providing an answer to this question is not as simple as it might seem, as there are so many factors that influence a child's behaviour. Cultural expectations, family traditions, intellectual disabilities, learning disorders, behavioural disorders, having experienced a trauma or being expected to act or behave as an adult and taking on adult responsibilities all influence how a child will behave. Parental separation and divorce can also be a major contributing factor to a child's behaviour. Constant conflict between warring parents often leaves the child feeling insecure and unsure about what will happen in their future. The child will often blame themselves for their parents' conflict and begin acting out their feelings; their behaviour resembles the turmoil they are feeling inside. These children can be difficult, argumentative and prone to having tantrums.

Even if the influences above are absent in the family, the simple fact is that children still do silly things, they can be selfish and self-centred, they will lie to you to get out of trouble, they will get angry and have a tantrum in the middle of the supermarket aisle because they can't have a lolly, they will ignore your instructions and argue with you, they will do everything they can to get out of bed – 'I'm hungry, I'm thirsty, I need to go to the toilet, I'm scared'. The adolescent will also have tantrums, they will yell at you, walk off slamming doors behind them, and both the child and the adolescent will scream 'I hate you!' when they are in trouble for doing something wrong.

Some parents have sometimes misunderstood the title of this session as they think I mean they should accept their child's problematic behaviour. This couldn't be further from the truth. This chapter concentrates on teaching parents to recognize and accept that their child will engage in 'childish' behaviour for a period of time. They will do and say 'silly' things and they will over-react emotionally and behave in a way that is … childish.

ACCEPTING CHILDREN'S EMOTIONS

Accepting children's emotions, or the way in which a child might try to express their emotions, is really about accepting that the child has a whole range of feelings and has the right to express those feelings in a supportive and safe environment. Parents can find it very difficult to tolerate their child expressing strong negative emotions such as anger, disappointment, frustration, fear or sadness and, unfortunately, they can respond in a manner where they may prevent their child's efforts to express their feelings. This often equates to parents pressuring their child to suppress their negative emotions. Parents' efforts at containing or controlling their child's emotional expressions can be varied. It may not sound all that bad – such as the traditional 'There, there don't cry' – or it may escalate to where the parent might angrily respond to their child with 'Cut it out, I'm sick of you carrying on!' or use emotional manipulation. When asking the parents why they find it difficult to cope with their child expressing strong emotions, one of the more common answers I'm given is that a distressed or angry child tends to distress the parents. Not to mention that a whingeing, whining child might get on their nerves after a while. So parents, to stop their own discomfort and emotion, try to contain their child's emotions in order to reduce the intense negative arousal they experience. Other parents have suggested that if it was just a matter of expressing their feelings it wouldn't be a problem, but that their child often becomes aggressive, destructive or abusive. This behaviour will be covered in depth in Chapter 9 on discipline.

Children need to learn how to safely and appropriately express all of their feelings, and parents who actively seek to suppress a child's emotions can cause greater problems for their child later in life. Further, forbidding a child to express their feelings is a form of authoritarian parenting. You may remember that authoritarian parents suppress a child's self-expression (see Chapter 2). Accepting children's emotions means simply sitting with your child and permitting them to express both positive and negative emotions in an understanding and supportive manner. It means taking the opportunity to teach your child about different emotions and how to express them safely without concern of reproach from you. You may recall Chapter 3 focusing on active and reflective listening where you were given some practical listening skills and ways to engage your child in conversation. This chapter takes those skills one step further so that the focus is on the emotional content or feeling state of your child.

ACCEPTING YOUR CHILD'S FEELINGS

So how do you show your child you are accepting their feelings in a supportive and understanding way? You need to allow your child to express all their feelings and respond to them at an appropriate moment. Then practise the following points.

1. Understand that even though permitting your child to express very strong negative emotions may be difficult for you, it is an opportunity for both of you to become close.
2. Using your active and reflective listening skills, try to understand what they are saying to you, what meaning or value is attached, and how your child feels about the situation. This will also help your child find the right words to label the emotion they are experiencing. You can help them label the emotions.
3. Sometimes children will tell you a story that doesn't seem to make sense or really sound that drastic. To understand what your child is feeling or the importance of the story for your child, the golden rule is to put their story back into your world. For example, your child may tell you they had an argument with their best friend at school and they are no longer friends. The risk here is to dismiss this event as trivial. But think for a moment about a friend who you may have spent a lot of time with, a friend who had the same likes and dislikes as yourself, a friend who

liked you regardless of your weaknesses and strengths and who shared many laughs with you. How would you feel if you lost that friendship due to a seemingly trivial argument? How would you feel if while trying to talk to your spouse about how you felt they dismissed this loss of friendship as trivial? Would you want to go back and try to talk to your spouse again the next time your feelings were hurt? Remember to walk a mile in your child's shoes without judging or dismissing their feelings, rather listening empathically and validating their feelings.

4. If you are unsure of the emotion/s your child is experiencing, just ask. Your child is not expecting you to be the expert and when you ask what feeling your child is experiencing you are saying, 'I'm here with you, I'm listening to you and I care about you and how you are feeling'.
5. This is also the time for teaching appropriate boundaries when expressing strong negative feelings. This can be achieved without suppressing your child's feelings. For example, you can inform your child that it is okay to feel an emotion such as anger, and it okay to express that feeling, but it is *not* okay to verbally abuse you or others or to punch walls or throw objects. This also helps your child to feel 'safe' with that feeling and reinforces that you are capable of dealing with their feelings. This can create an opportunity for both of you to seek strategies to solve the problem. The issue of setting appropriate behavioural boundaries and reinforcing those boundaries will be covered in Chapter 9 on appropriate discipline.

6. You need to reflect your child's feelings in a supportive and understanding manner even if in the first instance you don't understand why your child is expressing such feelings. Checking the detail of your child's story can be accomplished with greater success when they are not flooded with negative feelings. When your child has calmed down you would take advantage of the active and reflective listening skills to gather any relevant details of your child's story. This can help you understand where they are at emotionally and can guide you on how to respond to your child's emotional state in an appropriate manner.

ACCEPTING CHILDREN'S BEHAVIOUR

'How stupid can you be? All I asked you to do is get that [meal] out of the freezer. You're useless.' **(Mother of a fifteen-year-old boy)**

Parents need to be aware that children from the very young to the adolescent will often communicate their feelings behaviourally because of their developmental immaturity. Take, for instance, the following report from a concerned mother referring to her eight-year-old son whose grandmother was coming to visit. According to the mother, the grandmother visited with the family once a year. The mother opened our discussion with the following: '*I don't know what to do with him anymore: I mean, he can be so naughty. The other day when he found out his Nanna was coming to visit he ran around the house squealing and was jumping up and down on our bed.*'

The mother was so angry with her son for his exuberant behaviour that she punished him by taking away his favourite toys for two weeks. What this shows quite clearly is that a child is acting out what they are feeling in the only way they can at that age. It is important to be aware of this and it will help you begin to learn and understand what your child might be trying to tell you. Ask yourself a couple of simple questions: Is my child's behaviour potentially masking something else? Is my child trying to tell me something through their behaviour?

Accepting children's behaviour is simply accepting they are children and will engage in childish behaviour; it does not mean excusing misbehaviour. Accepting a child's behaviour is simply permitting a child to be a child and to enjoy 'childish' ways without criticism or punishment. It simply means children will engage in 'childish' behaviour and do 'silly' things like squeal with excitement, giggle and laugh, cry when they stub their toe, play with dolls when they are twelve or thirteen years old, or sleep with a teddy bear longer than *you* may think they should. Use active and reflective listening skills to get a clearer insight into your child's behaviour, opening lines of communication and helping your child to express their feelings effectively, appropriately and safely, no matter how old they are.

EMOTIONAL INTELLIGENCE

Emotional intelligence is another term that gets used quite a bit, but what exactly does it mean? Essentially emotional intelligence refers to a set of skills that enables us to navigate the world of feelings and emotions. These skills include the ability to sense an emotion in your body, the deliberate use of language to express that emotion, the ability to contain the emotion and communicate it in an appropriate way that suits the current context of the individual, and being able to choose one emotion over another. Emotional intelligence means we can process an emotion, let it go and allow ourselves time to feel. Emotional intelligence underscores intimacy, security and safe vulnerability in relationships and gives us the ability to:

- lead wisely or follow with grace
- give and receive love and support
- listen and sense empathically the emotions of others.

In a nutshell, emotional intelligence means that the individual is learning to recognize their own emotional state and the slight differences within those emotions; for example, recognizing that anger and feeling annoyed might be on the same emotional continuum, but are not the same emotion. Emotional intelligence means being able to think about a particular emotion, to label that emotion and be able to put it into words and express it safely and effectively. It also means being aware of the cause and effect or knowing what caused the emotion and being able to recognize emotional states in other people. Young children through to adolescents find navigating all the various feeling states that we experience very difficult to manage. Young children may feel strong emotions but often don't know how to express their emotions in an appropriate manner. The younger child is still just learning they have emotions with all the associated variations, they're simply not able to 'control' the expression of these feelings as an adult would. While the adolescent may be more mature, they too are still developing emotional intelligence and are also struggling with sudden changes in mood, which can take them by surprise.

Emotional intelligence is considered to be the cornerstone of all relationships as it enables close, loving and supportive relationships. It enables us to create, maintain and participate meaningfully in relationships, and professionals are keenly aware that emotional intelligence begins to develop in childhood. It is vitally important to remember that not only do children have a very limited range of emotional knowledge – that is, knowing and recognizing their emotions – but they also experience a lot of difficulty understanding their emotions and expressing their feeling states. Such developmental limitations further help to explain why children who are lacking in emotional knowledge and language skills may be more likely to act out their feeling states inappropriately through their behaviour. The lack of emotional knowledge children experience is a major reason why it is so important to learn and continually practise active and reflective listening skills.

As I've mentioned before, children need to learn emotional intelligence for their own healthy development and for the best chance of maturing into a well-adjusted adult. But where do children go to learn emotional intelligence? Do we send them to the school chaplain or school counsellor, to a paediatrician or psychologist or to a child psychiatrist? Sure, these are options but children actually learn emotional intelligence from you. Your own emotional intelligence has such an incredible influence on your children; it also plays a central role in their emotional health. Professionals know that undeveloped emotional intelligence in parents can have a lasting negative impact on their children. We know, for instance, that emotional intelligence is essential for developing people skills and for managing personal relationships. We also know that emotional intelligence is critical to your child's emotional, psychological and physical well-being.

Parents are powerful models for their children. Most people are aware that children watch their parents and learn by their parents' example how to act and react to situations, people and events. This also means that children learn about feelings and how to use them, how to handle them and how to express them. For example, one father was telling me about a time when he saw this very principle in action. One day the father had been doing some maintenance work inside the house and opened the back door so he could return his tools to the shed. Just as he was walking out the door with his hands full of tools, the door closed and hit him on the side of the head. The father yelled out in pain, 'Stupid bloody door!' A few minutes later he came back into the house through the back door. As he walked inside the house his two-year-old daughter grabbed the back door and slammed it shut, yelling out 'Bloody door!' She imitated her father's verbal and behavioural example of what emotions to express when things go wrong and the particular way in which he expressed that emotion.

It's a simple point that your level of emotional intelligence or lack thereof will *directly* influence your child through the way in which you verbally respond to situations and *indirectly* by the way in which you behave in any given situation.

Undeveloped or underdeveloped emotional intelligence in children has been linked to the following:

- Aggressive behaviour.
- Poor occupational or work prospects.
- Experiencing problems with and being unhappy in relationships.
- Addictions and gambling problems.

- A greater risk of developing depression and having higher rates of depression, adolescent suicide rates and anxiety disorders.
- An increase in eating disorders in children and adults.
- Stress.
- A tendency towards becoming a school, and potentially a workplace, bully.

Basically, children who have poor emotional intelligence are at a greater risk of misunderstanding other people's emotions. This means a child can become angry at another person because they have a tendency to attribute hostile emotions to others even when this is simply not the case.

On the other hand, emotionally intelligent children are:

- More likely to experience greater academic achievement.
- Less likely to become a school bully.
- Less likely to develop childhood behavioural disorders such as Oppositional Defiance Disorder or Conduct Disorder.
- Much better at problem solving in their emotional life.

It is widely accepted that teaching children emotional intelligence tends to naturally help them develop empathy because they are able to identify their emotions, which helps them relate to the people around them.

Parental emotional intelligence is one of those factors that can have a significant influence over your child. Parental emotional intelligence can also encourage a healthy and secure parent–child relationship and can directly encourage the development of emotional intelligence in your children. Following, you will find a few of the benefits for children who have emotionally intelligent parents.

A MOTHER'S EMOTIONAL INTELLIGENCE AND HER CHILD

Here are some of the benefits children experience as a result of mothers who develop emotional intelligence. Mothers who spend time with their children talking about their emotions in an open and honest way tend to have preschool children who have an advanced ability in being able to understand their own emotions as well as other people's emotions. Mothers who share positive feelings with their children tend to influence the development of their child's conscience and this creates a far greater moral understanding in that child.

However, mothers who are often angry, particularly with their children, are influencing their child's ability to empathize so that their child is less empathic and more often angry and defiant.

FATHER'S EMOTIONAL INTELLIGENCE AND HIS CHILDREN

Fathers who talk about their feelings and safely express their feelings tend to have a very positive influence over their children's emotional development. These children are in tune with their emotions, tend to be really well liked by their peers, experience academic success and are able to establish secure relationships with others.

However, if the father has poor emotional intelligence his children will more likely struggle in school, fight and argue more with their friends, and have poor health.

BENEFITS OF BOTH PARENTS TEACHING EMOTIONAL INTELLIGENCE

Children raised in homes where both parents are developing their own emotional intelligence and are concerned with teaching and guiding their children to develop emotional intelligence have children who are really quite resilient. Yes, these children still experience sadness and anger and can feel scared when faced with difficult circumstances, but not only are they better able to handle emotional situations but they:

- Have better physical health.
- Tend to do better academically compared to children whose parents aren't helping to develop their emotional intelligence.
- Get along really well with their friends.
- Have fewer behavioural problems.
- Are less likely to commit acts of violence.
- Experience fewer negative feelings and experience far more positive feelings.
- Are much healthier emotionally.
- Can calm and quieten themselves down emotionally.
- Are better able to handle distressing situations.

Emotional intelligence has even been shown to protect children from the devastating effects parental conflict and separation and/or divorce can have on them such as struggling academically, aggression and problems with their friendships.

Emotional intelligence is incredibly important because it creates the possibility for you to respond appropriately to what your child is telling you and to empathize with them, and it helps you to set very clear boundaries of acceptable behaviour with your child without turning to punishing or shaming them into compliance. If children are to develop a trusting, loving and lasting relationship with their parents, they must be given the opportunity to develop emotional intelligence. If a parent is to teach their child emotional intelligence, it makes perfect sense they would require a certain level of mastery over their own feelings. Sadly, this is not always the case. Many parents, particularly fathers, appear to have a restricted range of emotional knowledge and understanding and are really quite poor at appropriately expressing their feeling states. It seems that for men a number of negative emotions such as sadness, disappointment, frustration and rejection are all expressed as anger. I'm sure each of us can look back over our childhood years and recall sad events when our parents didn't respond to us in the manner we wanted. Some adults I see in my clinic recall incredibly painful childhood memories that are full of emotional, physical and sexual abuse or outright rejection from their parents.

If you have been hurt, rejected or let down by your own parents then you will understand the following questions.

- What is so important about parents developing emotional intelligence?
- Why would learning about emotional intelligence be in a parenting course?

I've said that emotional intelligence is the cornerstone of all relationships; it allows us to both give and receive love and support. Relationships cannot be intimate if they cannot grow or if they exist without a thorough knowledge and understanding of our loved ones' innermost worlds.

Professionals who work with families know that emotional intelligence also reduces many explosive episodes because, as a parent, your own emotional intelligence means you are aware of your child's feelings, you are able to empathize with them, soothe them at the right time and guide and teach them. Children with aggressive, non-compliant and explosive behaviour often have delays in language and as a result have a very limited vocabulary range to talk about their feelings effectively. Unfortunately, this contributes to children experiencing further difficulties in regulating the way in which they might respond across various situations. The connection is clear: children who severely lack the ability to effectively and appropriately express a range of feelings are at risk of explosive and defiant behaviour.

So how does emotional intelligence reduce behavioural problems? Teaching children how to accurately identify their emotions and to accurately label and express their own feelings as well as identify and understand others' feelings is recognized as one of the most appropriate forms of intervention that has been shown to reduce conduct problems. If they have learned emotional intelligence they are far more able to regulate their emotional states and talk about how they feel and why they feel that way, and this in itself reduces explosive and defiant behaviour. There are a number of ways in which this happens.

- Emotional intelligence provides us with the ability to correctly identify exactly what skills we need to not only understand but experience our feelings in the most adaptive manner.
- As emotional intelligence is also the ability to monitor not only our own feelings but to recognize the feelings of others, it means we can discriminate different emotions, and then draw upon that information as a means of understanding and guiding our thinking and behaviour. It helps us to respond to various situations in an acceptable way.
- Emotional intelligence means we have the ability to control our impulses, or begin developing self-control and thus delay the desire for immediate gratification.
- Emotional intelligence develops perseverance and self-motivation.
- Emotional intelligence helps us roll with the ups and downs of life as well as helping us to get along well with others.

EXPRESS YOURSELF – DEVELOPING EMOTIONAL INTELLIGENCE

Some parents find it difficult to accept strong emotions from their children. Many parents have told me that their parents would not allow them to express any emotions, let alone strong negative emotions such as anger. One adult male told me that, 'My parents would not permit me to display my emotions, and I was never permitted to talk about how I felt. Now, I don't know what I feel. I just can't seem to process my emotions. Recently my uncle died. At the funeral there was not a dry eye anywhere, but I couldn't cry.' Parents restricting or forbidding their children from expressing their various emotional states in a safe way run the risk of undermining their child's emotional development or emotional intelligence.

DEVELOPING EMOTIONAL INTELLIGENCE IN YOUR CHILD

Teaching children emotional intelligence can happen by using a number of different approaches. One of the most effective ways of instructing your child is taking advantage of 'in-the-moment teaching'. However, before launching into teaching your child emotional intelligence there are some simple ground rules you need to be aware of.

First, develop your own emotional intelligence so that you can develop an awareness of your child's emotions. There are plenty of really good books about emotional intelligence written by professionals who specialize in this area. I know it can be very difficult as parents to effectively, openly and safely express your own emotions in front of your children. But you must also realize that expressing your emotions in front of your child means you will be accountable to your child for not only expressing various emotional states safely and appropriately but also for labelling and effectively verbalizing those emotional states.

Second, a parent talking about their own feelings is incredibly helpful for their child's own emotional development. This is because you are actually teaching your child the 'how to's' of talking about emotions. The more time you spend talking about your emotions and the emotions of other family members, the more your child will learn how to describe their own emotional states. They learn ways of regulating their emotions, they learn how to regulate and control their focus on their own emotions and those of others, and they learn how to appraise their emotional responses and their emotional expression. To help you with this, consider the following points:

- Understand that whatever emotion your child is expressing, it is an opportunity for you to teach them further and to build a close relationship with them.
- Take every opportunity to use the active and reflective listening skills to help your child find the right words to label that feeling they are having.
- Listen empathetically and be sure to validate your child's feelings.
- Be sure your child understands there are limits on how to express their feelings. For instance, this is where you might use 'It's okay for you to feel angry, but it is not okay for you to [swear, throw things, punch walls, scream at me].'

It is a sad fact that there are parents who do not or will not take the time to teach their children emotional intelligence. After reading this chapter you would agree this really is doing your own child a disservice and runs the risk of creating potentially lifelong effects.

Teaching children how to correctly identify various emotions or to begin developing emotional intelligence can be achieved in a number of ways, including various mediums:

- Encourage your child to talk about their feelings. You can use examples to teach them the most appropriate way to respond to different situations such as events that might normally upset your child.
- If your child does not have the vocabulary range to label their emotion, they cannot effectively and safely express that emotion. One way you can aid your child's emotional intelligence development is to teach them feeling words. This can be achieved in a number of ways. The most obvious way is constant verbal instruction from you or you can try to label your child's apparent feeling state. You may recall that putting a feeling word into your response teaches your child what their current feeling might be. This approach also provides a connection between an emotion and the label, and allows your child to identify an emotion and to effectively verbalize and describe that emotion. Some ways of using feeling words include:
    - 'It looks like/sounds like you're angry at the moment.'
    - 'That must have been very disappointing for you.'
    - 'I understand you must be feeling angry right now about –'
    - 'It must have been very difficult for you. I guess you're feeling angry about it.'
    - 'I guess you must be feeling very proud of yourself.'
    - 'You look/sound really excited about that.'

- For the younger child, you can use the various forms of 'feelings vocabulary charts' that list numerous feeling words and pairs them with facial expressions. You can present the chart to your child and ask if they understand the feeling words. You can then teach your child the meaning of each word on the feelings chart. You can buy charts that have cartoon faces on them that illustrate different emotional expressions. Or search the internet to find some 'emotional faces' illustrations when you need them.
- For the younger child you can show them facial expressions in child-friendly magazines or children's storybooks. Turn to your child and say something along the lines of 'Have a look at this person's face. What do you think they are feeling?' If your child gets it wrong, don't immediately correct them. Praise your child for trying. Encourage them with 'Have another look at the person's face – what else do you think they could be feeling?' If your child still gets it wrong, encourage again and offer a suggestion.
- Once your child gets the idea of what you are asking of them you can extend this and also ask your child, 'How come that person might be feeling that way?' This is teaching cause and effect.
- The next step is to ask, 'What is this person thinking?'
- When at a shopping centre ask your child to look at someone passing by and ask them, 'What do you think that person is feeling?'
- As you are a powerful role model for your child (more discussion on parental modelling occurs in Chapter 6), you have the opportunity to effectively communicate and model appropriate emotional and behavioural expressions

to your child. If you have a tendency to suppress your own and your child's feelings, chances are your child will learn this is the appropriate manner in which to deal with emotions. However, if you are used to expressing your emotions in a healthy and safe way, the chances are your child will learn to do the same.

When you and your child have that emotional connection, you are even more invested in their lives and can therefore assert a stronger influence. You can be tough and set the rules when there is a need for toughness, and you are in a much better position to discuss your expectations of your child (more specifically the *behaviour* you expect of them). You are able to talk with them when they try to shirk their responsibilities and you are able to demand they live up to those responsibilities. You are able to effectively and with a great deal more success set limits. You can tell them when they have disappointed your expectations or let you down when you know they can do better. And because you have an emotional connection with your child, your words matter. They care about what you think and they don't want to let you down. Teaching your child emotional intelligence may help you guide and motivate your child.

ACCEPTING EMOTIONS AND DEVELOPING EMOTIONAL INTELLIGENCE HOMEWORK

In this chapter you have learned about the importance of accepting your child's feelings and behaviour. Most parents find it extremely difficult to accept or even permit their child to express very strong negative emotions such as anger or disappointment. However, in order for a child to learn how to express emotions safely and appropriately, it is vital they are given the opportunity to do this in the safety of their home. It is equally important to remember that accepting your child's behaviour *is not* accepting bad behaviour; it is simply accepting they are children, and need to act like children with all their immaturities and squeals of excitement.

It is important to remember that, if expressing strong feelings is not usually permitted in your family, your child may take a little time to respond. That's okay – persist! Take some time to think about the following questions and activities.

1. Do you allow your child to express all of their feelings? Provide some reasons for your answer.
2. If the opportunity arises during the week, make an effort to permit your child to express their feelings to you. If you think such an opportunity is unlikely to occur, have a go at asking your child how they might 'feel' about certain global topics like climate change?
3. Take note of how *you* felt during this time.
4. Did you notice any changes in your child's behaviour after they were permitted to express negative emotions?

And to help with developing your own emotional intelligence, consider what you have learned in this chapter and ask yourself the following questions:

1. Based on the information you have read in this chapter would you classify yourself as an 'emotionally intelligent individual'? Provide some reasons for your answer.

2. List five ways you can further develop your own emotional intelligence.
3. Provide three examples of how you attempted to further develop your own emotional intelligence.
4. List five ways you can further develop your child's emotional intelligence.
5. Provide five examples of how you aided your child's emotional intelligence.

Note: Always remember to practise active and reflective listening skills.

SIX

Parental Modelling

As a parent, you will often serve as an inadvertent example to your child. A child will model himself after you in many areas: how you deal with frustration, settle disagreements and cope with not being able to have the things that you want, to name just three.
– Lawrence Balter, 1989

From infancy children are taught how to become productive and mature members of their family and society as a whole by their legal guardians – their parents. This socialization or teaching instructs children about what behaviours are acceptable in their family, school and their wider community. Apart from using verbal instructions, parents can use a range of methods to teach and instruct their children about the behaviours that are acceptable in their home, school and in public. Indirect methods such as a parent modelling desired or appropriate behaviour is considered to be a powerful and influential way to teach and instruct children.

The point of this chapter is simply to show that you are not only an appropriate model for your child, but that you recognize and accept you are actually accountable to your child for your behaviour. To do anything else is to adopt the authoritarian parenting style of 'do as I say, not as I do'. In my experience it is often quite confronting for parents when they begin to develop an awareness of how their parenting skills (or lack thereof) may very well influence and reinforce the very behaviours they find difficult to manage in their children. This is because children learn through the natural processes of observation and imitation. Furthermore, as parents work through this session one of the greatest difficulties they face is coming to accept the realization that they are also accountable to their children for their own actions and attitudes. To make this a little clearer, consider the following questions:

- What messages are you sending your child through your behaviour?
- Is your child's behaviour simply mimicking your own behaviour?
- Is your child learning appropriate behavioural and emotional expression from you?
- What principles are you teaching your child through your attitudes and approach to life?

Children look to you as the adult, the parent, to learn what responses, attitudes and behaviours are acceptable across varied situations and events.

Parents who are verbally or physically aggressive model this behaviour to their children. Parents who use corporal punishment, manipulation, threats and shaming toward their child or toward others may very well be providing permission for their child to act in a similar manner. However, parental modelling is not restricted to such obvious and overt behaviours as corporal punishment or using guilt to manipulate a child. Children also learn from your attitudes, your approach to handling difficult situations, the way you go about resolving conflict, even the way in which you may speak to your spouse or other family members. Below are just a few examples of how parents model attitudes and behaviour to their children across various situations.

BEHAVIOURAL EXAMPLES

The mother of an eight-year-old boy and four-year-old girl came to see me with concerns about her son's behaviour. According to the mother, 'He gets really angry and throws the rubbish bin, pushes over the [dining] chairs, he pushes over the dining table. He's just like his father.' It turns out her husband was a violent alcoholic who would throw all manner of things at her and the children when he was angry.

A mother of an eleven-year-old boy said, 'He tries to lord it over me. When I try to talk to him about his behaviour he talks over the top of me in an aggressive manner. This is exactly how his father talks to me. He grew up in a physically violent home. His father would also belittle his mother and sister … now he is just like his father. He struts around the home as though he owns it. He is physically aggressive toward his mother and verbally belittles his sister.'

These behavioural examples are straightforward and reasonably obvious and so are the lessons the children are learning from them. But what about this example? The parents have had an argument. The mother and father have been yelling and swearing at each other. Dad leaves and walks into the living room where he finds his two young boys sitting on the floor using the PlayStation. As the father storms across floor his foot gets tangled in the console cords. He turns and kicks the PlayStation across the room, yelling at the boys because they are in his way.

What is the lesson the children have been taught? Later on, when one of the boys got angry he kicked the PlayStation across the floor and smashed it.

What about attitudes? What might your child be learning from your attitudes?

EXAMPLES OF MODELLING ATTITUDES

Parental modelling is not just restricted to behaviours. One woman told me that her husband told her it was her duty to always look her best and that she must wear fine clothes and make-up every day, and she was to greet him at the door dressed in lingerie when he arrived home from work each day. Apparently the husband also expected his wife to be a stay-at-home mother and housekeeper: completing all the housework each day, paying all necessary household bills, doing the weekly shopping, taking their three boys to after-school sports, and having his evening meal cooked and ready to eat when he arrived home from work. If she failed in any of these chores or if he was for some reason annoyed or agitated he was quick to berate or criticize her. He frequently spoke to her disrespectfully and thought it was amusing when she complained to him about how their three boys spoke to her in the same manner. What do you think the attitudes of this husband were towards his wife and women in general? What message was he sending his sons about the role of women, and the way in which women ought to be treated? What is this father teaching his children?

A seven-year-old child turns to an adult and calls out, 'Loser, loser!' The adult turns to the child and replies, 'You shouldn't say things like that.' The child looks straight at the adult and again sings out, 'Loser, loser!' The adult responds to the child again, saying, 'No, don't say that,' and then turns to the mother to suggest, 'You shouldn't allow your child to say things like that.' The mother of the child turns to the adult and angrily says, 'I'll teach my kid whatever I like.' Again, ask yourself what attitudes this mother is teaching her child.

Take a look at your behaviours and think about how they are seen by your child. Ask yourself the following questions:

- What behaviours do I want to teach my child?
- What behaviours or attitudes do I want my child to imitate or learn from me?
- What behaviours or attitudes am I actually teaching my child?
- Do I provide appropriate verbal instruction of the behaviours I expect from my child?
- Do I model that behaviour?
- Have I made myself accountable to my child for my behaviour?
- Am I prepared to apologize to my child when necessary and actually use the word 'sorry'?

Sometimes parents can be unaware that they are actually modelling inappropriate attitudes and behaviours to their children. If you find yourself in this situation and are wondering whether you are modelling appropriate behaviours and attitudes, a good place to start is looking at your child's problematic behaviour and assess whether there are similarities to your own behaviour. Here's a question I pose to every parent I meet with in my clinic: If you are modelling inappropriate behaviour (or attitudes) to your child, what right do you have to discipline (or reprimand) them when through your very behaviour you have told them the behaviour is acceptable? This is little more than 'do as I say, not as I do'. In other words you are practising authoritarian parenting and are a hypocrite.

And one more example. Imagine your boss at work was taking property from the premises without permission. You see him doing this and he makes an excuse that it is only small things like a carton of milk, a packet of biscuits or a pack of toilet rolls. Then one day your spouse asks you to pick up some milk on the way home from work. Knowing you don't have time to stop at the busy shops on the way home you go to the staffroom kitchen and take a carton of milk from the fridge. You intend to replace the milk the following day, but before you do your boss calls you into his office and fires you for stealing company property. You are shocked and indignant and inform the boss you have seen him doing the very same thing. He simply responds, 'That's different and besides I always replace what I take.' Your boss justifies his behaviour, the very behaviour you have just been fired over. How would you feel? The very person doing the very same thing has just fired you. How might you respond to your now former boss? Does this sound fair to you, does it sound hypocritical and a bit like 'do as I say, not as I do'?

The following characteristics will serve a parent well as a model for their child:

- Being a warm and responsive parent. This simply means showing your child love, affection and acceptance. Being responsive means setting time aside for your child when they need to be with you or to talk to you or to express their needs and to provide support, love and care when they need it. You are increasing the chances your child will respond to you in the manner you have modelled.
- Parental competence and power is attractive to children. Parents who are competent in being decisive are very often respected by their children. Parents who are easily persuaded by their child's misbehaviour when they make an unfavourable decision may appear incompetent and weak to the child and children do not generally respect such a parent.
- Consistency between assertions and behaviour. This is simply doing what you say. When you say one thing and do another you are being inconsistent with your assertions and your actions.
- Appropriate modelling can teach a child to inhibit unfavourable acts. Research has found that a parent who clearly states the reason for refraining from an unfavourable act is very effective in teaching their child self-restraint. The child can call on this explanation for self-restraint when they might encounter a similar situation in the future. The results of research focusing on appropriate modelling indicate that where children

are not only informed by the parent of what behaviour is appropriate, but further witness their parent modelling that appropriate behaviour, the children will more likely take on board that behaviour.

- Actions speak louder than words. When a child experiences the 'do as I say, not as I do' attitude, the child will more likely follow the parent's behavioural example. Simply put, when a child is aware of contradictions between what a parent demands of them and a parent's own behaviour, the child is less likely to comply with the parental demand for certain behaviour.

Chapter 5 discussed the importance of developing emotional intelligence. The final goal of this chapter is to encourage, teach and give you permission to be 'real' in front of your child. It might come as a surprise to you that your child already knows you; they know your faults, your limitations and your strengths. Being real with your child is being open with them and allowing yourself to express your emotions in various situations. Children need to see their parents as real people who experience real emotions and who navigate both the situation and the emotion. What a powerful opportunity to model emotional intelligence to your child; what a wonderful opportunity for your child to not only learn to recognize various emotional states, but to learn how to appropriately express those emotions. Given this parenting program is primarily for the parents of children with problematic behaviour, this is also an opportunity for you to honestly and openly discuss how your child's behaviour has a negative impact on others.

EXPRESSING YOUR EMOTIONS IN A HEALTHY MANNER

Your child needs to see you express all emotions in a healthy manner. The following ideas will give you guidance.

- Discuss with your child your feelings about the situation or their problematic behaviour and label your feelings. But *never* express disappointment in your child. Make sure you distinguish between the child and their behaviour.
- Discuss how your child's behaviour has had a negative impact on you.
- Do not blame your child for 'making' you feel a certain way. Like it or not, you are responsible for your own feelings and you are responsible for how you express them.
- Be prepared to listen to your child without interruption.
- Parents can intervene and begin to positively influence and change their child's aggressive responses by changing their own hostility and aggression and by discussing with their children that the violent or aggressive acts they are observing and imitating are not 'realistic or adaptive'. Parents can also get on with the job of teaching their children appropriate behavioural responses to various social situations that may trigger the child's inappropriate response or are typically handled poorly by the child.
- Be prepared to apologize to your child. One of the most powerful and healing words is a heartfelt 'sorry'. Saying you are sorry can cover a multitude of sins, heal broken hearts and repair troubled relationships. Parents know

they are not perfect in their parenting efforts. If your child is truly allowed to express their thoughts and feelings, in confidence and without fear of reprimand, they are able to express those moments when you may have offended them. If you were to respond in love and apologize for any offence you may have committed your relationship with your child will likely be strengthened. Both of you then have the opportunity to discuss the situation together, and you have a further opportunity to learn more about your child's inner world. Your child's feelings and thoughts are validated and therefore your child will more likely continue to express their feelings in the future. This, in turn, encourages the development of emotional intelligence in your child. However, if you respond harshly to your child or fail to respond to their feelings, they are less likely to risk expressing their feelings a second time.

- Ask yourself how you would feel if you tried to talk to your spouse after they had offended you and their response was, 'Don't be silly' or 'You're just being stupid' or 'You're just being over sensitive' or their attitude towards you sent the message that it really wasn't a big deal to them. How might this approach from your spouse influence the quality of your relationship?

PARENTAL MODELLING AND DEVELOPING HOMEWORK

This chapter was all about how you as a parent model to your child various forms of behaviour, thinking styles and reaction styles, interpersonal relationships, and communication styles with same-sex and opposite-sex friends and family. You found out about how you, as a parent, must become accountable for your own actions, not only what you do but also what you say. You discovered that if your child is practising inappropriate behaviour they could be copying you. Finally, you got to understand that the attitude of 'do as I say, not as I do' is not only contradictory in practise, but is also the authoritarian style of parenting. This hypocritical behaviour will only result in your child disrespecting you. Remember, children are more likely to copy *what* you *do*, rather than *do* what you *say*!

This homework is about being brutally honest and asking yourself the question: *'If my child is learning life from me, am I being an appropriate model?'* Think about the behaviours you model to your child, both good and bad. Also, remember to continue practising active and reflective listening skills.

1. Record three positive behaviours you model to your child.
2. Record three positive attitudes you model to your child.
3. Record negative behaviours and attitudes you model to your child.

SEVEN

Praise, Encouragement and Recognition

Praise is a wonderful teaching tool when it is specific and descriptive and genuine. It is also most impacting when praise is related to the child's efforts, not just the successes.
– Dr Cheryl Rode

Children of all ages need praise, encouragement and recognition. Our children are exposed to so much negativity every day at school and in mainstream and social media that they really don't need to hear it coming from you too. This chapter is about changing the negativity that can develop in the parent–child relationship by recognizing and encouraging your child's efforts and compliant behaviour.

This chapter also covers the topic of using basic manners with your child. For instance, parents ought to be mindful to use simple words such as 'thank you' and 'please' with their child. A simple thank you for completing a task or complying with a demand recognizes the effort your child has made and takes an opportunity to encourage your child. Praise is especially important for a child – for anyone really. It is particularly important for you to be prepared to praise, encourage and recognize your child and their behaviour during the time when the discipline program (see Chapter 9) is being established in your home. For example, if your child is attempting to control their behaviour – even if they are not completely successful – it is important for you to recognize the effort your child has made in attempting to control their undesirable behaviour. This serves a number of purposes. First, your child may feel encouraged in their efforts to control their behaviour and will more likely continue to repeat this positive approach to behavioural control. Second, rather than focusing on your child's negative behaviour, you are beginning to instruct your child on acceptable and appropriate behaviour. Finally, rather than being overwhelmed by the often negative exchanges between you and your child, praise can change the dynamics between the parent and child and serve to strengthen the parent–child relationship.

Everyone likes some form of recognition for their efforts, both in their professional and private lives; adults are not exempt from this general rule. For example, imagine you were asked by a friend to help them move house on a Saturday. You had a fun-filled family day planned, but because your friend was begging for your help, you postponed your family day and agreed to help your friend. You arrive at your friend's place early Saturday morning and begin packing boxes, loading heavy furniture in to the removalist truck and unloading that same truck at their new home. Finally, after a long day of packing and lifting heavy boxes and furniture you decide it's time to go home. You approach your friend and tell them how tired you are and that you are going home. But the only thing your friend says to you is, 'Oh, okay, bye.' No 'thank you' for your help, no recognition at all for the effort you put in, just 'bye'. How would you feel? A little put out perhaps, a little offended that your efforts were not recognized? What if this same friend came back to you a week later and asked for your help again, this time to collect more furniture from a storage facility they had used to store their excess furniture. Would you be as willing to rearrange your weekend again to help your friend a second time? The principle of praise and recognition is no different for children. Why should they try so hard to do the right thing all the time without any recognition? One five-year-old child captured this notion at bedtime as he knelt beside his bed for his nightly prayers, saying, 'Dear God, what's the point of being good if nobody knows!'

However, it is just as important not to praise your child for their efforts or successes alone. This can send the message to your child that they are only worthy of your attention, your love and admiration, or only acceptable to you, when they do as they are told or continue to achieve. Children can be deeply encouraged by realistic and timely support from their parents. Praise and encouragement can be delivered when your child has not come first in a race or has not achieved the highest results on an exam or might have fallen short of the desired behaviour. You can take the opportunity to comment on your child's efforts and to confirm unconditional love and acceptance. Praise and encouragement are another way of telling your child 'I love you and I care about you. I want to share in your successes and your failures. In fact, it's you I care about most, not your successes or your failures.'

While praise and encouragement are an integral part of parenting and an important part of the child's life, it must be delivered at an appropriate time as children know when they have not succeeded or completed a task as well as they could have or as well as other children. Unwarranted praise runs the risk of becoming meaningless. Equally, missing the opportunity to praise or encourage your child means you could be missing an opportunity to support them when they face difficult times. Again, walk in your child's shoes. Imagine that you were feeling down about a personal project you undertook because the end results were less than satisfactory. After you'd told your spouse how disappointed you felt, you received the response, 'Oh don't be silly, you're really great at that, you did a fantastic job, you should be proud of yourself.' No doubt you would see right through this and the praise would be meaningless to you. You might even become somewhat frustrated by this meaningless praise. The same principle applies to children.

TOO MUCH OR TOO LITTLE PRAISE

There have been some concerns raised in professional literature about the effects that too much praise lavished on children can have. The issue is that too much praise could be detrimental for the child as there is a risk they come to rely on praise and recognition for any and all of their efforts. Thus, the child will comply with demands only to receive recognition rather than learning the vital skill of self-control and self-regulation. If this pattern were to continue into adolescence and adulthood it could be a cause of great distress for the individual. For example, the teenager walking into their first job with the expectation that the employer will praise them for their efforts might well experience a lot of disappointment and frustration. It's unlikely that an employer will effusively praise the teenager for simply doing the job they are being paid to do.

Think of it this way: suppose you constantly praise your child for every single little thing they do, like washing the dishes after the evening meal, feeding the dog, making their bed, washing their hands, and so on. It would all become too much. Basic and everyday responsibilities like brushing your teeth and washing your hands after going to the toilet don't need to be praised. Again, be aware of the age-appropriate behaviour of your child. So for the toddler who packs up their toys at your request you might use words of encouragement, but the fifteen-year-old who showers after a sporting activity doesn't need to be praised.

I have read in a number of journal articles that some professionals argue *against* the use of praise as a positive reinforcement to change a child's difficult behaviour. It seems the issue of praise and recognition falls into two extreme camps of too much or not at all. In my opinion, children need praise and if it is genuine and delivered appropriately you are helping to build their self-esteem.

WHEN DO YOU PRAISE YOUR CHILD?

The next question is when should you praise your child? If praise is genuine, specific and earned there are not enough opportunities to praise your child. There are several different ways to deliver praise, though. Following are some suggestions:

- Praise for success. It is important to recognize your child's successes and praise and encourage them appropriately. For example, 'Good job, well done'.
- Praise for the effort the child puts in. For example, 'I'm proud of the effort you put in, good effort, well done'.

- This approach to praise also includes a realistic approach to a child's failures. It is okay to recognize that your child might not have succeeded at a task, and it is very important for children to learn how to deal with disappointments and failures. Some children can try really hard with their school homework or in their chosen sport but not do so well. What's important is that you make a positive comment about the effort they put in. Otherwise you can run the risk of achievement-based praise only, which means that you are telling your child that they are only acceptable to you when they are achieving.
- Be realistic with your child about their struggles or their failures but still encourage them. For example, 'I know you're struggling a bit with science, and I'm proud of the effort you put in. How about we do it together?' or 'I know you didn't do as well as you had hoped for, and I understand you feel disappointed about that, but I am proud of how hard you tried.'
- Be genuine. Children can see right through false, forced or half-hearted and insincere praise. These forms of praise are meaningless and run the risk of telling your child 'I don't really mean what I'm saying'. If your child has made a genuine attempt or put in the effort, make a suitable comment. Keep in mind, too, that praise is not a precursor for the 'real message'. Don't mix praise or encouragement with a negative word. For example, 'What a good effort on the science exam, but if you had studied harder you could have done better.' The real message here is 'you have failed'.

- Resist the temptation of 'I told you so'. Children know when they have not put in the effort. Approaching a child with an attitude of 'I told you so' runs the risk of crushing their spirit.
- When your child is misbehaving, be sure to separate the behaviour from your child's character or personality. For instance, saying to your child, 'You're a liar' or 'You're a bad boy' suggests the child is that very behaviour. The child then runs the risk of developing a belief that they are bad or not good enough, that they are a failure or worthless. Separating the behaviour from the child's character or personality means that you label and describe only the undesirable behaviour. For instance, rather than saying 'You are a bad boy for lying' you might say 'Lying is a completely unacceptable behaviour.' Conversely, when you praise your child, direct the praise to their personality or their character. In other words, praise the person and the behaviour. For instance, 'You are such a good boy for not lying, I am so proud of you.'

Praise, encouragement and recognition for success, effort and failure are not enough. Children also need to hear words of love, comfort and support regularly.

Some parents have told me they rarely use words of praise or encouragement with their child and have never said 'I love you'. In my experience, men find this particular session quite difficult to come to terms with and the most common response I hear is, 'I don't know how to praise him as my dad never praised me.' I've also been told many times by men 'She knows I love her', or

'He knows I'm proud of him'. The question 'How does your child know this?' is often met with the response of 'They just do.' But unless you tell your child that you love them or that you are proud of them, how will they know? There is also an issue of imbalance here. If you point out your child's failures (for example, bad or disappointing behaviour) and don't praise or encourage them, all you are ever doing is focusing on the negative. How do you think that makes your child feel?

There have also been a number of occasions when parents have reported they have never cuddled their child. Let me be blunt: this is usually more about issues the parent is facing and rarely has anything to do with the child. You are the parent, you chose to be a parent and, like it or not, parenting comes with tremendous responsibilities. One of those responsibilities is to encourage your child and to teach them how to manage hurts, frustrations and disappointments with your loving support, and that includes cuddling them or holding the older child close to you. Praise, encouragement and physical displays of love convey such powerful messages of acceptance regardless of whether your child fails or succeeds. If praising, encouraging and recognizing your child's efforts are foreign to you, get in there and deal with it, as this reinforcing behaviour will go a long way towards helping you to repair the parent–child relationship. Don't miss an opportunity because you don't know how to cuddle and praise your child. Jump on the internet, go to the library, talk to your health professional – there is no excuse.

There is one more issue that can be as problematic as it is desirable. The problem with using 'excellent' as a form of praise is simply that there is no higher form of praise. For example, your child places fifth in a school cross-country run. You praise your child for their effort and respond, 'Well done, that's excellent.'

Then two weeks later your child competes in another school cross-country run and places first. What then? What higher form of praise can you provide? As you begin to implement the discipline program, you will notice your child will make certain attempts to control their behaviour. You take the opportunity to praise them for their efforts, but if you use 'excellent' at the early attempts, there is nothing higher to encourage your child with when they do succeed at controlling their problematic behaviour.

Finally, two small but very powerful words: 'thank you'. Just as parents are not their children's slaves, children are not slaves to their parents. How many commands, directions or demands do you make of your child each day? Of these, how many times have you stopped and said a simple thank you? It's a radical idea, I know, but if I asked you to make me a coffee and I didn't say thank you, I'm sure you would consider me rude. But what if I demanded that you make me coffee several times a day and I never once said thank you? Would you begin to feel a little angry with me? One of the things I teach couples going through relationship counselling is to do everything they can to avoid taking each other for granted. A simple 'thank you' for the effort put in to cook you a meal or wash your clothes or for the maintenance around the house goes a long way to saying 'I love you and I appreciate the effort you put in'. The same applies to children: they appreciate being thanked for their efforts.

So how do praise and recognition work to change a child's difficult behaviour? Essentially it comes down to consequences. Any behaviour, positive or negative, is changed by consequences. Most of us are aware that when the term 'consequence' is used it seems to refer to a negative response, such as discipline for some undesirable behaviour. However, consequences can be positive as well. Positive consequences such as praise and recognition for a desired behaviour increase the likelihood that it will happen again. This reinforces a positive association in the child's mind between a desired behaviour and its positive consequence. The trick is that the positive consequence needs to be delivered as close as possible to the time when the desired behaviour occurs. This shapes the child's behaviour towards the desired behaviour.

When your child starts to change their misbehaviour and the desired behaviour becomes more and more evident, the desired behaviour still needs positive consequences to continue reinforcing the desired behaviour. Otherwise there is a risk the misbehaviour can re-emerge.

PRAISE, ENCOURAGEMENT AND RECOGNITION HOMEWORK

This chapter has shown you how important it is to encourage your child, recognize your child's efforts and respond with encouragement and praise. It is important to praise your child for their efforts and failures, not just their successes. Finally, you also learned about how important it is to say a simple thank you to your child after complying with any request.

1. During the following week look for ways to appropriately praise your child.
2. During the following week try to find three ways to encourage your child's efforts.
3. During the following week remember to thank your child for complying with your requests.
4. Make sure your efforts are sincere because your child will see right through fake praise.

EIGHT

Developing Empathy and Moral Behaviour

The opposite of anger is not calmness, it's empathy.
– Mehmet Oz

We have talked about the importance of children developing emotional intelligence: the ability to detect, understand, label, discuss and appropriately respond to the feelings of others. Remember how emotional intelligence is closely linked to the development of empathy? In fact, emotional intelligence is considered to be the prerequisite to empathy. Empathy is defined as an individual having an emotional response to the emotional state of another or the situation they are in. Empathy contains both cognitive and emotional dimensions – that is, to understand how another person is feeling and to share in their emotional state, we put ourselves in another person's position to understand their situation, what their motives are and get an idea of why they are behaving the way they are. Empathy is not only a feeling or an emotional response to the plight of another person. Empathy also influences affective and cognitive processes.

Most of us would be aware of the affective or the emotional component of empathy as we 'feel' what the other person is feeling and we then might respond to that person with a sense of compassion for them. The cognitive component of empathy is about being able to understand or really appreciate another person's perspective or having the ability to understand another person's emotions.

So what has all this got to do with parenting difficult children? When you are able to cognitively understand and tolerate another person's perspective you are less likely to become aggressive with that person. For example, through my work with returned soldiers I've heard many, many stories. Apart from the tragic situations these men and women have lived through, one of the more common stories I've heard is the difficulty these soldiers experienced when returning home from active service. During World War II, many Australian soldiers were captured and detained in Japanese prisoner-of-war camps in South-East Asia. Once the war was over, the surviving soldiers were released from these camps and returned home. When they arrived back home, they were expected to get on with life and pick up where they had left off before the war. They had to 'forget' what had happened to them and to their fellow soldiers killed in action. The cognitive element of empathy is being able to understand the soldier's perspective or understanding their position – Japan was our enemy, they were trying to kill us, to destroy our way of life, we went to war to protect you, we suffered at their hands and now you want us to be friends? The affective element of empathy would be you experiencing the same or very close to the same emotion that these soldiers felt at the loss of their mates, the confusion of the situation, the anger, and even the sense of betrayal they may have felt.

However, understanding someone else's feelings (cognitive empathy) is not enough on its own to develop appropriate behaviour; rather it is the integration of both affective and cognitive empathy that produces pro-social behaviour. This is because aggressive children typically experience a great deal of difficulty with taking another person's perspective and recognizing emotions in other people (thus the reason why teaching children emotional intelligence is such an integral part of any parenting program).

The integration of both components of cognitive and emotional empathy is known to inhibit and reduce aggressive behaviour, as the aggressor tries to avoid their own emotional distress caused by their behaviour or to reduce their victim's emotional and/or physical pain. Affective and cognitive empathy actually helps the aggressor to feel or experience the pain they are causing their victim.

So how does this relate to overall behaviour, particularly the behaviour of children?

- People who are highly empathic are able to foresee how their own poor behaviour will negatively impact those around them. What this tells us is that children who are able to respond emotionally to other people's feelings are far less likely to show aggressive or delinquent behaviour.
- Empathy predicts selfless behaviours, it promotes prosocial behaviour in the classroom, acts against antisocial behaviour and reduces criminal behaviour.

- Children who are empathetic are more popular with their peers and are more outgoing and sensitive to the needs of others, are emotionally stable and perform better at school.

In the long run, when a child experiences the distress they have caused others because of their aggression, they are less likely to continue their aggressive behaviour and are actually more likely to help that person (one of the reasons why parents can discuss the effects their child's behaviour has had on them).

HOW TO DEVELOP EMPATHY IN YOUR CHILD

Before we move onto the 'how to' of developing empathy in your child, you need to know that there are a number of parenting practices and parenting behaviours that will actually block, stunt or inhibit a child from developing empathy. These include:

- Parental emotional neglect, often seen in authoritarian and uninvolved parenting.
- Threatening your child and physically punishing them in an effort to control their behaviour.
- Inconsistent reactions to the way your child might try to express their emotional needs.
- Rejecting or withdrawing from your child's emotional needs.
- Domestic violence.
- Bribing children to behave the way the parent wants them to.

Equally there are parenting practices that promote the healthy development of empathy that include:

- Being responsive to your child's needs and not acting in a punitive manner.
- Talking openly with your child about how their behaviour has a direct effect on you and those around them.
- Explaining why your child's behaviour has been hurtful to you or to others and discussing more appropriate ways of behaving in similar situations.
- Teaching your child how and when to apologize for their inappropriate behaviour.
- Teaching your child that they can actually make people happy by being kind, thoughtful and generous.
- Teaching your child emotional intelligence by modelling caring, empathic behaviour.

MORAL DEVELOPMENT

Let's turn to the issue of morality and how children develop morals. Have you ever thought about why there are people who hold themselves to a higher sense of morality while others choose to live with few if any moral standards at all? For some people, one of the most important things in life is not only living in accordance with the law but reaching out and touching the lives of other people through self-sacrifice, through caring and giving, and living by high moral standards. For others, simply obeying the law and caring for their loved ones is enough. They don't seem overly concerned with moral codes or laws. Then there are some people who act in a self-serving, selfish manner, who will do whatever it takes to make sure their own needs are met even if that means hurting other people and taking advantage of them. In the pursuit of satisfying their own needs some people will even step outside the boundaries of the law.

Morality is considered to be multifaceted with two important components, known as cognitive morality and affective or emotional morality. Cognitive morality simply refers to the way we *think* about rules around ethical behaviour, while affective morality refers to the way we *feel* about moral issues. But before we consider further the attributes of morality, we need to have a better understanding of how children develop moral behaviour. Any discussion around children developing morals must take into account two of the most influential scholars in modern history who have painstakingly studied moral development in children: Jean Piaget and Lawrence Kohlberg.

Through his work, Piaget identified two stages of how moral reasoning develops in children. The first stage is known as heteronomy, where children are essentially governed by what others determine as right and wrong. In this instance, the parents influence a child's understanding of right and wrong, as the child does not yet have the capacity to differentiate between them. For example, the child begins learning moral behaviour when the parent informs them it is wrong to steal or to lie. In the early years, the child accepts the parent's word and follows their instructions. As children grow older and begin to mature they enter Piaget's second stage of autonomy, where they begin making decisions for themselves about what is right and wrong based on their own views. The autonomy stage of moral development is no longer influenced by the child's parents;

rather the decisions are based on the child's strong sense of right and wrong and is further developed through interaction with their peers.

Similarly to Piaget, Lawrence Kohlberg also believed that children's moral development happened in stages. For Kohlberg there were three stages or levels including the Pre-conventional level, Conventional level and the Post-conventional level. Kohlberg believed that the Pre-conventional level is at a time of development in the child's life when they are self-centred and are incapable of understanding or recognizing other people's needs or even that other people actually have needs. The Pre-conventional stage is also evidenced by children's understanding of right and wrong or good and bad and is based on punishments and rewards. Essentially, this means that while children might have an understanding of right and wrong, it may still be developing, and before engaging in an action the child will weigh up the *consequences* for that action first. As children enter the Conventional level they start becoming aware of other people's interests and their understanding of being good is now conforming to the moral demands of society. The Post-conventional stage is evident from about the age of thirteen years onwards. This stage shows us that the child has now developed a moral system, as morals are now very personal and independent of the child's instructions for acceptable behaviour. The Pre-conventional and Conventional stage of moral development show us that a child's behaviour is motivated by outside forces (for example, parents, other adults, negative consequences). The Post-conventional stage demonstrates that moral behaviour is now intrinsically motivated by the child's convictions and it is now a personal characteristic. What all this means is that children are constantly learning from their parents what is and what is not acceptable behaviour. Through this moral instruction children eventually develop morals with a conviction of the importance of following their morals. This means then that the child begins to consider the moral aspects of their behaviour and is making decisions to act in a moral way that is independent of extrinsic forces in their life such as parents, peers, larger society or negative consequences.

However, more recently, other theories of moral development have suggested that early morality really depends on an intertwining between a child's self-awareness and their knowledge of right and wrong and their understanding of social standards and rules about appropriate behaviour. A child begins to develop what is known as higher order emotions such as guilt or shame. The emergence of these emotions suggests that the child is becoming self-conscious as they are beginning to understand and evaluate themselves. This process of self-evaluation is fundamental to the development of guilt and shame. Such emotions are considered to be vital to the development of moral behaviour. But the child also begins to experience additional unpleasant feelings other than just guilt and shame when they are misbehaving. Essentially the range of negative or unpleasant emotions in the context of 'being naughty' is considered to be adaptive as it reinforces to the child that such behaviour is unacceptable. As such, unpleasant emotions in the context of misbehaviour serve to prohibit socially unacceptable behaviour. Further, our judgments about good and evil or right and wrong are also influenced by empathy and disgust, which also assist in developing moral behaviour.

COGNITIVE AND AFFECTIVE MORALITY

Cognitive morality is how a person thinks about rules around ethical behaviour while affective morality refers to how a person feels about moral issues. Cognitive morality is really about moral reasoning that helps us determine right from wrong based on rules and laws. It also refers to the ability of 'cognitive perspective taking', which enables a person to recognize what another person is feeling without actually sympathizing or feeling the other person's emotional state. It is basically head knowledge. You can see the other person might be upset, but you don't sympathize with them or feel what they are feeling. Affective morality is void of and independent from moral reasoning and refers to emotional morality, which directs a person's behaviour based on how they feel about a given situation leading to moral behaviour. This is where guilt, shame and empathy come into morality as they are considered to be the most important emotions underpinning morality. What all this actually tells us is that cognitive morality, or simply knowing right from wrong, is not enough on its own to guide moral behaviour. Instead, the development of morality requires both cognitive and affective attributes, and it is the combination of both these attributes that is found to guide moral behaviour. The absence of affective morality has been linked to:

- Selfish, self-serving behaviour.
- Aggressive behaviour.
- Bullying behaviour.
- Antisocial behaviour.
- Delinquency.
- Lacking the ability to feel what others feel and to care about others.

- A defined persistent temperamental pattern that reflects a lack of empathy, guilt, remorse, and a disregard of others.
- Difficulty with resisting temptation (for example, antisocial behaviour).

How to help develop moral behaviour in your child

Moral reasoning or the ability of the child to make moral judgments or decisions about what is right or wrong is linked to parenting styles. As a parent you need to be prepared and willing to invest the time and energy needed to teach, instruct and demonstrate to your child moral and empathic behaviour.

Before you can begin, you need to decide what morals you would like your child to learn. Once you have clearly decided what morals you would like to teach your child you need to sit down and have a discussion with them. In age-appropriate language and using examples if possible you would inform your child about what you are now expecting of them. You would explain your moral rules in as much detail as necessary. However, as already discussed, the adage 'do as I say, not as I do' will not work and runs the risk of your child developing contempt for you and what you say. Put simply, you cannot demand moral behaviour from your child and then act immorally when it suits you. A child's moral development begins in the home by listening to your instruction and watching what you do. It is important to model the behaviour that you want your child to learn. So, let's get started.

- You would have noticed that empathy is one of the attributes underpinning morality. Teach your child emotional intelligence and empathy (focus on how another person might feel).

- Discuss your own emotions and the emotions of other family members. This assists in developing moral sensitivity to others.
- Develop appropriate behavioural boundaries and insist your child comply, and explain the differences between 'good' behaviour and 'bad' behaviour and how their behaviour (good or bad) affects others.
- Teach your child to be kind and compassionate.
- Teach them about justice, rights and equality. Teach them to care about others (for example, become involved in community welfare, visit the elderly, teach them about the sacrifice of soldiers).
- Model the behaviour you want.

But the teaching does not stop there. Just because you have taken the time to talk about and model morality with your child, it does not mean that they will not need further instruction and advice as they come across new situations, peer pressure to act immorally, and temptations to behave in a manner you may believe is immoral. Children require parents who are constantly willing to advise, discuss, teach and guide their children in all manner of behaviour.

DEVELOPING EMPATHY AND MORAL BEHAVIOUR HOMEWORK

This chapter discussed the importance of child empathy and morality in reducing aggressive, defiant and antisocial behaviour and we have discussed ways to help you in assisting the development of empathy and morality in your child. Now it's time to begin that process.

1. Decide what morals are important to you. Then decide how you will begin teaching your child about empathy and morality.
2. Provide two examples of how you taught your child about empathy and morality during the past week.
3. Provide two examples of how you demonstrated or modelled both empathy and morality for your child during the past week.

Section 2

LEARNING HOW TO EFFECTIVELY DISCIPLINE YOUR CHILD

NINE

Learning Effective and Appropriate Discipline

Good discipline is more than just punishing or laying down the law. It is liking children and letting them see that they are liked. It is caring enough about them to provide good, clear rules for their protection. – Jeannette W. Galambos

If you have not read the preceding chapters, go no further. You will need that information under your belt before focusing on this chapter. This book was never intended to teach parents new ways of getting the upper hand over their child. Equally, if you have read the preceding chapters and have not been practising all the parenting skills, you should not attempt to put into place with your child the discipline strategies that follow. The reason for this is simple. If the parent–child relationship is fractured or struggling, you run the risk of causing further harm to the relationship and becoming little more than an authoritarian parent. This can and often does increase difficult and aggressive or non-compliant behaviour in children, particularly boys, and is said to increase and condone aggression toward others.

Discipline must be clearly distinguished from punishment. Parents who use punishment often argue it is appropriate and necessary to control a child's misbehaviour. Take for instance the mother of a five-year-old boy discussing the issue of punishment.

> *'I'm the authoritarian here and he needs to learn that. A good smack never hurt anyone. My parents smacked me as a child. Society has slowly eroded parents' rights to discipline their children. If we had smacked our children maybe there wouldn't be so much crime in society.'*

However, more often than not punishment is little more than an angry parent lashing out at their child for some unacceptable behaviour. Punishment often (but not always) involves some form of corporal punishment such as smacking, slapping, hitting, pushing, kicking or biting. Professional literature describes corporal punishment as hitting, striking, wounding or bruising your child as a means of discipline or punishment.

For example, when discussing appropriate consequences for a child's inappropriate behaviour, one father who had been bitten by his young autistic child informed me he had become enraged at his child's actions and, as a form of punishment to 'teach him what it feels like', he bit the child on the arm. The bite was delivered with such force that it left a noticeable bruise on the child's arm. So much so, the teachers noticed the bruise the next day and called child protective services. The father couldn't see anything wrong with his behaviour and argued, 'Well, he won't go biting me again, will he?' His action could be argued to be cruel and unusual punishment, and was treated and investigated as child abuse. This is *not* discipline, this is punishment and the reaction from an angry father was abusive. Parents can become emotionally aroused when their child is 'pushing all their buttons' and can be unaware of the force with which they are actually striking a child as opposed to how much force they think they are using.

There are many other problems with punishment. Professionals, laypeople and parents are increasingly questioning the long-term efficacy or its measured success. Apart from the very real risk of harming the child and the relationship becoming abusive, current research and actual experience informs us that smacking a child only modifies the behaviour in the short term or in that moment; it fails to modify a child's misbehaviour in the long term. Because a tired, exhausted and angry parent sees an immediate change in their child's behaviour, smacking or other forms of corporal punishment can become the preferred means of punishment. One very significant reason smacking does not work is because the smack itself does not help the child to internalize the 'lesson' or values or morals this form of 'discipline' is supposed to instil. If you don't believe this just ask yourself two simple questions.

1. Has smacking your child changed their behaviour in the long term?
2. After you have smacked your child, do you find some time later that they still do the same thing?

Discipline, on the other hand, is viewed as teaching, guiding, explaining and training the child 'in the ways he should go', not just when the child engages in misbehaviour. Prominent researchers have provided us with a clear distinction between discipline and punishment, suggesting that any form of effective discipline is a positive and beneficial way of deterring your child from unacceptable behaviour through the use of various consequences in conjunction with setting your child very clear boundaries for acceptable behaviour

Discipline has at its foundation absolute respect for the child with an understanding that while it may indeed incorporate negative consequences for a child's misbehaviour, such consequences only play a small role in modifying a child's misbehaviour overall (and the preceding chapters should be evidence of that). The discipline program discussed later on will show you how to clearly differentiate between discipline and punishment and will help you to step back from getting caught up in an emotionally charged situation when needing to discipline your child.

The following discipline program is designed to serve a number of purposes. First and foremost, it allows parents vital space from becoming emotionally involved and striking out in anger, thus not only potentially harming the child physically, but also potentially harming the parent–child relationship. Because parents are able to step back from an emotionally charged situation, discipline is managed in a controlled and calm way using consequences that are predetermined rather than an angry parent lashing out in desperation, trying to find some kind of punishment that will work. In other words, parents are given an opportunity to reduce their emotional and physical involvement in disciplining their children and focus on being able to respond in a calm and controlled manner.

INCONSISTENT DISCIPLINE

Children and adolescents become quite distressed by their out-of-control behaviour and feel so much more secure and happy when their parent takes control. You need to be aware, though, that there is a chance your child's problematic behaviour may increase or 'spike' when you first introduce this program. The reasons for this can be varied; however, it is imperative you are aware you must follow through with the discipline program as some children will challenge you and the program. It is as if your child is testing you to see if you really mean what you say. Be warned, if your child's misbehaviour spikes and you fail to enforce the program, your child's misbehaviour will be reinforced. If your child's misbehaviour does spike, don't give in, maintain your resolve and your determination, and simply continue the discipline program.

Sometimes the consequences may need to be adjusted or altered if the behaviour doesn't appear to be changing, but that's okay. Just keep on applying the discipline you have decided on. For example, one mother had the discipline program running for her son for two weeks. During the initial stages the mother noted her son's aggressive behaviour had decreased overall. However, the boy became involved in a fight at school and was suspended for three days. The mother had decided any form of aggressive behaviour (for example, hitting, kicking, throwing objects, swearing) would have a consequence of her son going to bed half an hour early that evening. Given the serious nature of fighting, the mother decided the assigned consequence was insufficient for the 'crime'. So the mother altered the consequence from half an hour early to bed to one hour early to bed for each of the days the child was suspended from school. She then contacted the school and requested the child be sent home with adequate homework to cover the three missed days at school. All electronics during the normal course of a school day were off limits to the child, who instead of having a mini holiday from school and homework, had to complete each day's assigned school work and see out the remaining normal school hours without being entertained by games or playing outside and without electronics.

DISCIPLINE: LISTING FIVE BEHAVIOURS

Your first step is to choose the five most troublesome behaviours shown by your child that need to be changed. Write them down under the heading, 'Behaviour' (for example, see Table 1 on the next page). No more than five behaviours should be listed as there is a risk of overwhelming your child with too many expected changes. On the flip side, it does not matter if fewer than five behaviours are listed. Essentially, the list of behaviours begins with the most troublesome behaviour and moves down to the least. For instance, any form of physical or verbal aggression would be positioned as the number one behaviour to be modified, with a clear understanding that it is completely unacceptable and will not be tolerated, whereas swearing might be placed in position two and so on.

TABLE 1 Behaviour

	Behaviour
1	**Aggression**
2	**Swearing**
3	
4	
5	

When I talk about listing behaviours that need to be changed, parents are often very quick to call out their child's problematic behaviour. However, mostly parents describe these behaviours in very generic terms. For example, parents will often cite aggressive behaviour as a major concern that needs to be changed (and rightly so). While there may be a general understanding of aggressive behaviour, this is just too vague as aggressive behaviour could be punching, kicking, biting, slapping, pushing, using inappropriate language, throwing objects, punching walls, breaking toys, taking toys from other children and so on. The same applies for non-aggressive behaviour such as lack of respect and non-compliant behaviour. While you may know what you mean by respect, there is a very good chance your child will not have the same understanding. Thus, it is important to break down the descriptions into actual behaviours. Essentially, what you will be doing is ensuring your child has a very clear understanding of the offensive behaviour that needs to be changed. Also, when it suits them, some children are experts at finding ways out of contracts for acceptable behaviour and will tell you, 'But that wasn't in our agreement.' So by listing physically aggressive acts you are making it clear there are no 'legal' loopholes. See Table 2 on the following page for an example of how to list aggressive behaviours.

TABLE 2 Behaviour continued

	Behaviour
1	**Aggression**
	• Hitting
	• Biting
	• Kicking
	• Punching holes in walls

If your child engages in both physical aggression and verbal abuse you would place these behaviours under the heading of aggression as these behaviours are completely unacceptable. In this instance, there may be a number of behaviours you want to see changed but just remember to limit the behaviours to a maximum of five. See Table 3 for an example of how to list both physical and verbal aggression.

TABLE 3 Behaviour – listing examples of each behaviour

	Behaviour
1	**Aggression** **• Hitting** **• Biting**
2	**Verbal abuse** **• Name calling** **• Demeaning/belittling language**
3	**Non-compliant behaviour** **• Refusing to do as we ask**

LIST FIVE CONSEQUENCES

Once you have worked out and listed your child's most problematic behaviours, the next step is to complete a comprehensive list of potential consequences. This simply requires you to make use of the many privileges that your child has a means of deterring unacceptable behaviour. I cannot stress enough, however, that under *no* circumstances are you to use a child's rights (for example, warmth, food, shelter, clothing, unconditional love, the right to be respected, the right to be safe, and so on) as consequences. However, there are many, many privileges you can use. The problem is that as privileges are a part of everyday life for many children it can be quite difficult to think of appropriate privileges to use as consequences.

Whatever consequences you decide on, they should suit the behaviour (as it were), and need to be harsh enough that they will serve as a permanent discouragement, but at the same time not be overwhelming for the child. For instance, one of the favourite consequences parents will use for younger and middle age children is the 'early to bed' consequence. If you have listed aggression or swearing at the top of the behavioural list, you will send your child to bed one half-hour early for each aggressive act. Essentially, the consequence should be tough enough to really matter to your child. For example, some parents have used their child's bicycle, other parents have used all electronic equipment (no television, computer games, etc.), or Lego. Ideally there should only be one fixed consequence per problematic behaviour. That is, it is not recommended to use the same consequence for different behaviours or to combine a number of consequences from the consequence list to use on a single behaviour. This is simply a matter of fairness and helps you to not react to misbehaviour and out of frustration use the harshest punishments listed for the lesser 'crimes'. It also further prevents the child from feeling overwhelmed by the consequences. However, where aggressive acts are listed, such as in Table 2, you can use the corresponding consequence as many times as needed. For example, hitting, bitting and kicking all come under the heading of physical aggression. Therefore, the consequence of sending the child to bed one half-hour early could be applied to each act of aggression. So your child could end up going to bed very early. One important point is to *never* send your child to bed without a meal.

A HELPFUL HINT TO KEEP ON TRACK

Over the years many parents have told me that when they apply this discipline program in their home, their child has responded with 'I don't care' after a consequence has been used. This is a very common approach from children who are trying to keep you from knowing just how much that consequence actually hurt. It is also quite common for a child to do this in an effort to throw you so that you think 'nothing works' and give up.

Many times parents have explained to me they have tried every form of discipline imaginable and nothing works. By this stage parents are at their wits' end and out of desperation often use lengthy bans on their child. That is, banning a child from an upcoming birthday party or banning them from gaming for the next two weeks and so on. However, this can create a sense of hopelessness and helplessness in your child, particularly if they continue to misbehave over that period of time. You get to a point where you feel as though you have nothing left to 'punish' your child with and this is where the risk of corporal punishment, shaming or rejecting your child becomes all too real and you can begin to feel like you're fighting a losing battle. But when this discipline program is up and running in your home there is one rule you must remember – the consequences you have decided on should last for no longer than 24 hours. This is because the consequences are not to be overwhelming for your child, and depending on the age of your child, they are unlikely to remember why they were punished in the first place some four weeks later.

There is also the issue that lengthy discipline is a constant reminder of wrongdoing on the part the child, and this can run the risk of shaming your child. Remember that earlier I said to try and walk a mile in your child's shoes? Well, here's how lengthy consequences might work for adults. Imagine that one day you said or did something that upset your spouse or best friend and four weeks later they were still not talking to you. How might you feel? Angry, annoyed, hurt, rejected? You might recognize the negative impact this continued punishment is having on you. How do you think this might influence your relationship with this person? It really is no different for a child. If we continue to punish a child, we run the risk of damaging the parent–child relationship and shaming the child.

Table 4 shows a completed version of listed behaviours and the subsequent consequences.

TABLE 4 Consequences

Top 5 Behaviours	Consequences
Aggression	
• **Hitting**	
• **Biting**	
• **Kicking**	Half an hour early to bed
Swearing	No television /phone/internet for a day
Lying	No electronic games
Arguing	No computer
Not going to bed	No Lego

DISCIPLINING THE YOUNGER CHILD

For the younger child it is recommended you use a time-out approach. This simply means placing a chair in the corner of a room where there are no distractions (for example, pictures, television, etc.) and having your child sit there for no more than 1 minute per year of life. For example, if your child is four years old they would sit on the time-out chair for no longer than 4 minutes. However, the time should be guided by the parent, and by the misbehaviour. For example, the parent of an aggressive four-year-old may have the child sit in the time-out chair for the entire 4 minutes but they may not need to sit in the chair for as long if it's for refusing to tidy up their toys.

Here is how it works:

- You will need to select an appropriate corner in your home to place the chair. Then you will explain to your child each step of time-out in an age-appropriate manner. Using appropriate examples, you would explain that when your child misbehaves (for example, hits out) they would be sent to the time-out chair.
- You then take your child to the time-out chair and have them sit on the chair while you explain the rules. For example, 'When you hit me, you will have to sit here until Mummy [or Daddy] comes to you. You are not to get off the chair until Mummy [or Daddy] comes to you.'
- When the time limit is up, you are to return to your child and explain again in simple terms why they were placed in time-out. At this point you can request an apology if the preceding misbehaviour necessitated such a response.

- The time-out approach is designed to protect the parent–child relationship, as when a child frequently displays aggressive or defiant behaviour, is angry, tired or exhausted, parents can be at risk of 'lashing out' in anger or frustration.
- By removing both child and parent from the situation not only is the child learning that misbehaviour has consequences, but you also have the opportunity to 'calm down' and to process your own emotions so that you can approach your child in a calm and controlled manner. It is vital you understand that once time-out is completed, that is the end of the consequences; you are not to remain angry with your child, nor can you later remind your child of their misbehaviour. Instead, you forgive them and continue the relationship in a loving and supportive manner. This is just a small part of what unconditional love really means.
- Before placing your child into time-out, you need to provide time for your child to try self-control or comply with your request. This step is exactly the same as for the older child. For example, 'If you don't pick up your toys you will be sent to time-out. One … Two … Three.' If your little one has not made an attempt to comply with your request in that time, you would escort them to the time-out chair.
- Does time-out work? Yes it does and it can be a very effective means of discipline. The mother of a four-year-old who frequently head-butted, kicked and punched used the time-out chair. After the child had been sent to time-out only twice, the child said to his mother, 'I no

want to sit in the chair, I good boy now.' The mother told me, 'He has not hit, kicked or head-butted me since.'

- But, just as with all forms of discipline, it can be ineffective if you don't follow through with it or only use it occasionally. Remember, you have listed your child's problematic behaviour that needs to change and turning a blind eye to it only reinforces that problem behaviour.

DISCIPLINING THE ADOLESCENT

The same principles of using privileges as consequences apply equally for the adolescent (and even the adult child at home) as they would for a younger child. Again, a consequence means removing a privilege of importance to the adolescent, and they have many privileges that can be used. Supposing your fifteen-year-old adolescent wags school – again. How do you discipline him in light of all the information you have read so far? The discipline program is about finding an appropriate consequence that has meaning to your child. For instance, some parents have not permitted their child to use screens (computer, internet, electronic games, mobile phone, etc.) unless it is for school use only, as all these items are privileges. With the adolescent you would also take the opportunity to teach them how their problematic behaviour is destructive and can have negative consequences for them and impact the parent–child relationship. For example, you might say something along the lines of 'I find it very hurtful when you say [ ] to me' or 'I find it very hurtful when you treat me this way. Why should I drive you to your friends' homes or to the movies or buy you expensive clothing or pay your mobile phone bills or cook you nice meals if you treat me in such a disrespectful manner? If you want me to continue doing these things for you, you will respect me in the manner that we have discussed.' Parents are not their children's slaves and children need to learn to respect all the things parents do for them as privileges not rights.

There are times when you may have to be tough with your decisions when it comes to disciplining the adolescent. Why should you cook them nice meals, buy takeaway for them, drive them to their friends' homes or wash their clothes when they insist on disrespecting you? Why should you allow them to use your electricity to play on their computer or watch their television in their room, and why should you have to pay their mobile phone expenses or allow them internet access on their mobile phone if they are aggressive or abusive towards you? A mother of a fifteen-year-old girl came to see me about her daughter's abusive behaviour towards her. The daughter was quite moody and, if feeling annoyed, she would swear at her mother and call her some incredibly hurtful names. But then the mother would drive her daughter anywhere she wanted to go as soon as the daughter demanded. She would drive her to parties and if the daughter rang her at 3 a.m. the mother would get out of bed and drive off to collect her daughter. Regardless of how the daughter treated her, the mother would always give her daughter whatever she wanted. When I told the mother it was time to stop giving her daughter everything she wanted and time to tell her daughter 'When you start respecting me I will start doing things for you', the mother refused and stopped coming for help.

I hope you can see that you are not bound to run around after your selfish, aggressive or abusive teenager and you are not bound to continue to give them all their wonderful privileges if they are not earning those privileges by respecting you. Yes, you are bound to ensure they are fed (but that doesn't mean they must eat the roast dinner you had; it does mean they can eat a bowl of broccoli instead), they are to be clothed (but you don't have to buy those expensive jeans or runners), they are to be warm, protected and loved but that doesn't mean you have to be their personal taxi or teller machine. It's simple: if the adolescent wants all these wonderful things from you, they can earn them or go without!

CONTINGENCY PLAN

Many parents have told me they have tried using privileges as consequences to curb their child's misbehaviour but have had little success. In my experience this is generally because once the child has misbehaved and the consequence is meted out, parents feel there is little more they can do if their child continues to misbehave. This is where a contingency plan is very helpful.

The contingency plan is really about effectively using the many privileges a child enjoys on a daily basis as a means of supporting the initial discipline program. After you have decided on the initial five consequences, it is time to develop a contingency list of *all* your child's privileges. For instance, privileges would include PlayStation, Game Boy, computer games, you or your spouse running the children to friends' places or buying takeaway food, renting DVDs, buying brand-name clothes, toys, etc. The list is endless and you need to make that list as large as possible (for example, listing at least twenty privileges). In my experience most parents find developing a contingency list somewhat difficult and often report they don't know what to write. To help parents develop such a list, I suggest they look around the house and in the child's room and make an itemized list of objects from most loved or valued to the least loved or valued. The contingency list is a back-up plan used for a very specific purpose.

Suppose for a moment you have placed hitting in position number one and swearing in position two on the behaviour list. Then in the adjoining consequence list you have placed going to bed a half-hour earlier for each hitting offence and the loss of all electronic gaming use for swearing. Your child comes home from school in a bad mood and you ask them to take the rubbish out. Your child turns and tells you to 'get lost'. You inform them that the behaviour is unacceptable and that they will now be losing all electronic game privileges. In a fit of anger your child kicks a wall. Now they receive a second consequence of going to bed half an hour earlier that night because they have been aggressive.

But what if your child continues to swear at you, what then? Have you exhausted all your options of applying discipline? The answer is no. Rather than entering a clash of wills that really serves no purpose, you now refer to the contingency list and, beginning at number one (for example, riding a bike, playing with Lego, etc.), simply and calmly state 'Because you choose to continue swearing at me you have lost the privilege of using your bike for 24 hours.' Depending on the response from your child you would simply work down the contingency list, removing each listed privilege as necessary. It has been my experience that when parents have had to refer to the contingency list – and have followed through with it – they have only had to use it once or twice, as the child soon learns that losing so many privileges for 24 hours is just not worth the effort.

FAMILY MEETINGS

Once you have completed the behaviour and consequence list, it's time to call a family meeting. In this family meeting you will sit down with your child with the behaviour and consequences list and explain what it all means, in simple terms. This is the reason why you had to be very clear about describing the behaviours you wanted modified. You need to inform your child of the behaviours that are upsetting and unacceptable and explain how the consequences will work. As James Dobson (1999) said, *'The child should know what is and is not acceptable behaviour before he is held accountable to those rules'.* At this point you can also ask your child if there are any problematic behaviours they are aware of, as some children are both aware of and concerned about their misbehaviour.

Recently I was talking with a teenager and his mother about his problematic behaviour at school. I said to the mother we might have to consider some consequences at home if these behaviours continued at school. The boy joined in the discussion and started listing behaviours he felt were unacceptable and gave his mother a couple of ideas for consequences.

Finally, effective parenting also teaches the child to be aware of how their behaviour impacts others. So during this family meeting you will also discuss with your child how their behaviour impacts you and the other members of the family. Some points to remember when using the discipline program are listed below.

- Once you have had your family meeting the time to turn a blind eye to problem behaviour has gone. For children in the category of behavioural disorders or explosive and defiant behaviour your involvement must be immediate. While there are instructions listed later in this chapter about the finer details of applying consequences, the thing to remember is not to put it off or pretend you didn't see it or hear it. Also, praise and recognition should be immediate.
- When your child engages in those unacceptable behaviours that need to be changed, there are a couple of things you need to do when it is time to use consequences. The first thing to remember is to use the words 'choose', 'chose' or 'choice'. This is because you are taking the opportunity to teach your child it is their choice to behave in that manner. The second thing to remember is to name the misbehaviour your child is engaging in. For example, if your child has kicked a wall you might say, 'Because you have chosen to kick the wall you will be going to bed one half-hour early tonight.'
- If your child engages in non-compliant behaviour you might respond with 'If you choose to continue this behaviour there will be no electronics.' For the younger child and even middle-age children you can count aloud to three, then if your child has not complied with your request apply the predetermined consequence. For any non-aggressive behaviour the child should have the opportunity to alter that behaviour prior to the consequences being applied by the parent. If there was to be an immediate consequence

without the preceding teaching of ownership of behaviour, you might run the risk of becoming authoritarian in applying the discipline and that may escalate the situation further. Finally, applying immediate consequences for non-aggressive behaviour does not allow the child to learn to self-regulate.

- Of course, any variation of these instructions is acceptable. However, you must remember aggressive acts are not to be tolerated and require an immediate consequence.
- This approach is designed to serve a number of purposes. First, by saying 'If you choose to continue to [unacceptable behaviour]' you teach your child they are making the choice to engage in a particular behaviour that is unacceptable. Your child is learning they can be in control of their behaviour and is therefore responsible and accountable for their behaviour. This is the beginning of learning self-control.
- Utilizing such phrases can provide you with some emotional distance from the situation. Giving yourself this distance prevents you from becoming emotionally overwhelmed and will allow you to stay in control of the situation and provide the ultimate opportunity of 'in the moment' teaching. That is, teaching your child about poor choices, consequences and appropriate behaviour. This is a vital life lesson for children.
- This is also an issue of helping your child develop self-control. Self-control is the current, trendy new term for what was once called strength of character. When children are learning self-control, they are also developing self-discipline and moral behaviour at the same time. Self-control, self-discipline and moral behaviour are considered

> to be the most important foundations to becoming a well-adjusted adult. This is because children are learning how to replace, restrain or stop socially unacceptable and undesirable behaviours. They are learning how to control their behaviour, thoughts and feelings.

Over the years many parents have asked me how to manage their child's misbehaviour outside the family home. As conduct problems in children tend be expressed across different situations and different environments such as the classroom, the school playground, grandparents' homes, friends' homes, or in the shopping centre and so on, having a discipline program that only addresses problematic behaviour in the family home is insufficient. The simplest answer is that the discipline program needs to be applied to each area of the child's life. For example, if your child is misbehaving at school, you may need to contact the classroom teacher and request to be informed of any misbehaviour from your child during the course of the day. Further, your child is to be informed that if you are contacted by their teacher they will be subjected to the designated consequence that evening at home. I often inform children of all ages that the discipline program will follow them everywhere they go. So if they misbehave at school not only will they suffer the consequences the teacher may dish out, but they will also have consequences at home. At the family meeting you must inform your child that the consequences are in place across all situations.

Finally, it is very important you remember that once the consequences have been applied, that is the end of the discipline. All too often a parent may remain angry with the child and can withhold love and affection. Apart from this being rejecting in nature, there is also a great risk of sending the underlying message to your child of 'You are only acceptable to me when you do what I want you to do'.

Once the desired behaviours become the norm, the initial problematic behaviours can be 'wiped' from the behavioural list to symbolize a clean slate. When it comes time for you to do this, make sure your child is with you and give them the opportunity to wipe off the behaviour themselves. If that initial troublesome behaviour returns, simply place it back on the board or if new problematic behaviour emerges, and after discussing it with your child, simply place that troublesome behaviour on the board.

KEEPING THE SLATE CLEAN

In my experience with this program, children will tear up or scribble all over the behaviour and consequences lists. I suggest you print out each individual list on an A4 piece of paper and just write the headings 'Behaviour' and 'Consequences' on it with the numbers 1 through 5. Laminate it and then you can write or wipe off any and all behaviours and consequences as necessary.

WHY AGGRESSION ATTRACTS THE HARSHEST CONSEQUENCE

Apart from obvious concerns such as the child injuring themself or seriously injuring another person, there are other concerns that must be addressed. It is completely unacceptable to turn a blind eye to aggression or violence in any form from children (or adults for that matter). We know that when aggressive children reach adolescence and adulthood, they have a higher risk of the following:

- Behaviours such as delinquency, violence and substance abuse.
- Developing depression.
- Being more likely to experience escalating academic problems and drop out of school.
- Early parenthood.
- Experiencing rejection by their peers.
- Becoming involved in criminal behaviour in adulthood.
- Experiencing adult mental illness.
- Displaying antisocial behaviour.

Aggressive, defiant or behaviourally disordered children need rules and boundaries just like every other child. In fact, it could be argued that these children, whose internal world might be absolute chaos, need it more than other children as boundaries provide stability for children. Keep in mind that appropriate discipline also helps children to take responsibility for their own behaviour.

SETTING AGE-APPROPRIATE CHORES

Each member of a family ought to be responsible and contribute to the smooth running of the family. This means children as well. Chores are really about teaching children responsibility and cooperation within the family unit instead of taking for granted that their mother (and sometimes father) will do everything for them. As part of a family unit, children must learn the responsibility of working together to support the family as a whole. Furthermore, the various chores a child can undertake can present an opportunity for them to learn how to clean their own home as adults, instead of expecting their spouse (usually the wife) to do it for them. A single mother of a thirteen-year-old boy told me he had to learn how to clean the lavatory and the bathroom sink. He was taught how to vacuum, cook meals and wash his clothes. While her son really didn't appreciate the idea, the mother believed that not only was this helpful to the family unit, but she was teaching him a valuable life lesson.

GENDER CHORES

Men, there is nothing more undermining, belittling and degrading to a woman to be told that because she is a stay-at-home mother she has to do all the cooking and cleaning and be responsible for the entire household while you justify your lack of help and support in the family home with the argument 'Well, I go to work'. It is poor parenting and can place enormous stress on the marital relationship. Furthermore, what messages are you sending your child about their mother and women in general! You chose to make a life with your spouse and you chose to have children. That means you chose the responsibility of building a family.

Most children are in a position to undertake chores around the house, from the young toddler learning to pack away toys to the middle-aged child loading the washing machine to the teenager watering plants. It is important you carefully choose chores your child is physically and safely able to complete. At this point it must be made clear that time-consuming chores or too many chores can be burdensome for children and can interfere with their after-school relaxation time and homework. It is recommended that children do no more than two to three chores per day. For instance, an eleven-year-old child can cope with putting out the rubbish and loading the washing machine daily. Again, you discuss chores with your child to get their ideas, collaboratively decide on reasonable daily chores your child can complete, and also discuss how chores benefit the whole family.

PATIENCE IS A VIRTUE

Be patient and take the time to teach your child how to do the chore properly. Be careful not to place too high an expectation on your child's early efforts. This can be damaging to a child's self-esteem and self-concept. For instance, one mother reported of her son's attempt at vacuuming their lounge room carpet that 'Oh, he never does it properly. I always have to go and vacuum after he's finished.' The son, who was sitting right next to his mother in my office, was looking down at the floor and responded with 'Yeah, I never do anything right.'

When a list of chores has been developed, it is time for you to write up that list under the heading 'Weekly Chores' as shown in Table 5.

TABLE 5 Weekly Chores

Weekly Chores
Load washing machine
Feed dog/cat
Put out rubbish
Sweep floors
Vacuum

Once the chores have been placed on the laminated Weekly Chores list, to help your child remember their responsibilities you can draw up a Daily Chores list.

TABLE 6 Daily Chores List

Johnny's Chore List		
Monday	**Feed dog**	**Putting clothes out to dry**
Tuesday	**Put out rubbish**	**Set dinner table**

Once you have discussed with your child the chores they are responsible for, it is a good idea for you to show them exactly how to do it from start to finish. Once you have shown them how to do the chore, have your child complete it while you are there to offer further advice and instruction as required. You may need to show your child how to do their chores several times before they really understand what is expected of them. Each chore should be broken down into parts.

Set age-appropriate chores. As your child matures the chores can be changed to more challenging ones. Again, chores are determined according to the child's age and abilities.

Teach the younger child how to complete one chore at a time. Instructing children on too many chores at once can become confusing and overwhelming for them. For younger children you may need to show your child a number of times how to complete that chore before moving on to the second one.

Parents can fall into the trap of constantly reminding their child to complete their chores. This approach simply moves the responsibility of completing chores from the child onto you. The chores have been printed and placed in a position in the house where your child can look at them. For the older child, completing their chores is part of them learning responsibility. However, younger children may need the parents to make a single reminder. If your child forgets or simply refuses to complete their chore, you would apply the appropriate consequence. For instance, refusing to complete a chore would come under defiant behaviour and you would apply the predetermined consequence for that behaviour.

Should the child forget or refuse to complete their chore, you are not to complete it for them. If you do, all you are teaching your child is that you do not mean what you say and if they hold out long enough you will complete their chores for them.

Remember to say a simple thank you once your child has completed their chore/s. Every member of the family needs to feel appreciated. It is a powerful encouragement to your child.

POCKET MONEY

Many parents suggest pocket money is a good idea and for many families pocket money is tied to household chores. However, many parents tend to struggle with how much pocket money to pay their child. Some parents pay their eleven-year-old child

₹1000 per week, while others pay ₹250 per week. The question of how much is too much or too little can be a difficult question to answer. Some general guidelines are listed below.

- Pocket money payments must *always* be within the parents' means.
- If you tie pocket money to chores, each completed chore should have a set monetary value.
- What is the average amount of pocket money your friends pay their children?

Many parents have told me their child simply refuses to complete any chores they have given them. It must be noted that there are consequences for the child who forgets or refuses to complete their chores. This issue is discussed in more detail on the following pages. Where pocket money is paid to your child, instruct them that each chore has a set monetary value. If the chore is not completed by the assigned time, the monetary value of that chore is deducted from their pocket money for that week. For instance, where a child is required to complete two chores per day (based on a five-day week) and receives ₹250 per week, the value of each chore would be ₹25. Where the child forgets or refuses to complete the required chore, ₹25 would be deducted from the child's pocket money for each chore for each day. Some parents have reported that when they have applied this consequence their child has immediately gone out and completed the assigned chore and then expected to receive the monetary value placed on that chore. Should the parents pay their child the monetary value of that chore? The answer is no. If your child forgets or refuses to complete their chore/s within the given timeframe, the monetary value for that chore is deducted from their pocket money. A really good way to get this message across to your younger child is to hold in front of them the money they would have earned and explain that because they have refused to do their chore they do not get the pocket money for that chore.

For the younger child, using visual keys can aid them to both remember their responsibilities and continue to be motivated to complete the assigned chores. This can be accomplished by paying the child their pocket money at the end of each job or at the end of the day. For instance, each chore might have a value of ₹10 or ₹25, which would be paid to the child at the completion of their assigned chore. Younger children really like having lots of coins as they think it means they have been given more money. For instance, a child may receive ₹25 per chore. You decide to pay your child after each job. Rather than give notes, you can ask your child if they would prefer ₹5 coins. Also for children with attentional disorders, paying them their pocket money at the end of each chore is a must. Trying to make them wait until the end of the week is not going to work in your favour.

As already mentioned, sometimes there need to be consequences for the child who totally refuses to take on the responsibility of completing their assigned chores. Remember, each member of the family is responsible for helping to support the family and, again, parents are not their children's slaves. It is totally unreasonable for the teenager to refuse to wash the evening meal dishes and then demand that their mother take them to their friend's place. Children do not respect you when you give in to their demands and allow them to shirk all their responsibilities. You might need to place non-compliance on the behaviour list and decide on an appropriate consequence.

Remember, though, that paying children pocket money for set chores is different to asking them to pitch in and help clean the house on a weekend because friends are coming for dinner. Children need to learn to work together for the common good of the family unit.

TABLE 7 Consequences for refusing chores

Top 5 Behaviours	Consequences
Aggression **Swearing** **Lying Arguing** **Not going to bed**	**Half an hour early to bed** **No television for the day** **No electronic games** **No computer** **Vacuum the house**
Chores	Rewards
Daily chores listed **Pocket money organized**	

Some parents have suggested that their child will refuse to complete their household chores once they have earned some money from previous jobs. The children seem to think they have earned enough money from household chores to retire from their responsibilities. A common attitude parents report from the child is 'I have enough money now so I don't have to do any more jobs'. If this is an issue in your home, there are a number of ways to stop it from happening.

- For children who *do not* have attentional disorders, you can withhold their pocket money until the end of the week. That way they only get paid when all their jobs are completed.

- Open a bank account in your child's name and have them accompany you to bank the total of their pocket money each week. This means they have no money in their hands.
- Withhold half of their pocket money and bank it for them.

Finally, earning pocket money can be a great opportunity for the child to learn how to handle money and to learn the value of money and that it is not easy to come by. We have to work hard for the money we earn and we are not prepared to waste it. This is a good principle for children to learn and there are a few things you can do to help develop a healthy respect for money.

- Don't give your child money whenever they want it.
- Don't give them an advance on their pocket money if you cannot trust them to complete their chores, and even if you can, don't make advanced payments a common thing.
- Don't lend them money unless you have clearly established the ways in which they will pay back their debt. This might be through completing extra chores around the house or paying a certain amount of their pocket money back to you each week.
- Sit and talk about finances with your child. However, don't burden them with your financial woes.
- Teach them the difference between purchasing good-quality items as opposed to cheap products that last about 10 minutes.
- Have them save their money to purchase items they really want. However, just because your child wants to purchase an item, that does not mean they have the right

to purchase items that are not suitable for them or items that contravene your family values and morals. Also, just because they purchased the item, that does not exclude it from being added to the consequences list. For example, if you have decided all electronics or screens are used as part of the consequences for misbehaviour and your child has purchased a new phone or tablet, it can still be added to the consequences list

- For the older child, teach them about wages and award rates, the cost of living (for example, food bills, utility costs, rent or mortgage payments), the principle behind borrowing money from financial institutions and how to manage and prioritize their wages. Older children need to understand that their local financial institution is not going to be impressed they did not pay their car loan because they wanted the latest mobile phone.

REWARDS

The topic of rewarding children for good behaviour has been a contentious issue in the professional world for some time. Some professionals advocate rewarding children when they have been well behaved, while others argue there are just too many problems associated with reward systems. The contention has come about because rewards can be used to buy a child's 'good' behaviour. Many times parents have told me they have made a bargain with their child that if they are good they will get them a special reward. One mother once told me they made a bargain with their son that if he was good for the following six months they would buy him a front-row ticket to the tennis final, while another mother of younger children told me that whenever they had to go to the shopping centre, she told them that if they were good she would buy them candy.

Buying children's good behaviour is wrong and a child will not develop respect for you for this. They may also simply learn to rely on rewards to guide their behaviour. The mother of the younger children went on to tell me that her children were beginning to demand more and larger treats and that if she said no they would have an all-out temper tantrum right there in the shopping centre. She was setting up a very unhealthy cycle. Rewards come *after* the behaviour, *after* the child has tried and is learning self-control and *after* they have demonstrated the responsibilities you are asking of them.

Rewards should never be money or expensive gifts. One teenager told his mother that if he was going to do the things she put on the behaviour list, then she could buy him a very expensive Xbox game. Needless to say he was not impressed when I told him to think again. Rewards can come in many ways, from thanking a child for completing a chore to occasionally throwing in a little extra pocket money for the way they have been getting in and helping you around the house, to setting up a tent in the living room and having a 'camp-in' with popcorn and a movie. The thing to remember, though, is not to put the rewards too far ahead. Six months ahead is not a good idea. Occasionally, you might offer a larger reward of taking your child to a movie or something of that nature. You may have noticed the general theme of this reward system is still very much centred on family time.

Following is a short list of possible rewards.

- Staying up a little later on weekends (not Sunday nights).
- Date with mother/father.
- Afternoon at the park.
- Swim at the local pool.
- Swim at the beach. Trip to library.
- Day out.
- Choice of dinner venue (occasionally).
- See a movie.
- Fast-food dinner (occasionally).
- A small inexpensive toy (for example, Transformers, Lego mini figures, crystals, rocks or gems, soft toys).

SCREEN TIME

Notice that increasing screen-time as a reward was not listed. It is generally considered in the professional field that children spend too much time on screens as it is. It has become such a problem that children are literally not learning vital social skills, are not learning how to navigate confrontations, are not learning appropriate assertiveness, are tending to isolate themselves in favour of their screen time, can be disconnected from their family and are generally losing the art of communication. I have had some parents tell me the only way their teenager communicates with them is via phone texting or via Facebook messages. I have been into people's homes where every single member of the family was using some form of screen at the same time. There is no communication or connectedness happening in that family.

FAQS

Q: What if my child keeps getting up from the time-out chair before the time limit is up?
A: The child is returned to the chair and the time count starts again, until the child has sat for the designated time.

Q: What happens when my child has been aggressive and we have to go out that night and they're meant to be in bed early?
A: Sometimes children will misbehave just before you head off to a meeting or to do the shopping, and the usual consequence is disrupted by the scheduled appointment. In such cases you would explain to the child their behaviour has been unacceptable, and while the usual consequence is unable to be applied in this instance another more fitting consequence will be used instead. Again, any consequence must match the misbehaviour and last no longer than 24 hours. In such an instance you can use a suitable consequence listed on the contingency list.

Q: What do I do when my child misbehaves when we're out, say at the shopping centre?
A: If misbehaviour is a common occurrence when you are out, take time before you head off to the shops to discuss with your child the expected behaviour from them while you are out. If your child does misbehave, return to the approach of 'If you choose to continue this behaviour you will [remind the child of the impending consequence that will be enforced]'. Alternatively, you might just stop your shopping, tell your child the shopping trip is over and return home and enforce the consequence. As much as it might be an inconvenience in the short term, the message

is 'Your misbehaviour will not be tolerated and you will not get away with it in public settings'.

Q: When I tell my child we will do something special together he can be really well behaved. But when we get back home he treats me so poorly that it makes me not want to do anything special with him again. What can I do?
A: Before you go out be very clear about what behaviour you are expecting from your child when you return home and explain that if your child misbehaves when you return home, there will be consequences (as recorded in the consequence list).

Q: The consequences we use are not working. She just doesn't seem to care what consequence we use; what do we do now?
A: It might be that the consequences you have chosen are not working because they have little meaning for your child. Remember that each consequence should be harsh enough to deter your child from engaging in those behaviours you want modified. Go back and rethink what privileges you have at your disposal that you can use and that are really quite meaningful to your child.

Q. My child will stop when I say 'If you choose to continue this behaviour there will be [the predetermined consequence]'. Then 5 minutes later he's doing it again and says 'I did stop'. What do I do?
A. Children are masters at finding 'loopholes' when it comes to any discipline program and they will try such tactics to confuse you and render your efforts useless. The simple fact is that your child is continuing the behaviour after being told to stop. Therefore, the predetermined consequence would apply. Remember not to get caught up in justifying the discipline program or arguing with

your child about why they are receiving a consequence. You are the parent: they do as you say.

Q: What if my child misbehaves all week? Does she still get a reward at the end of the week?
A: No, the child does not. The child learning to modify their behaviour earns these rewards.

Q: What if he only misbehaves a couple of times throughout the week; does he still miss out on his reward?
A: Some parents have a system where the child will have a couple of chances during the week before losing out on their weekly reward. For example, the child may have a consequence placed on them two or three times in the week before losing their reward.

Q: Is it the same for the monthly rewards?
A: In principle, yes. This means that children can have two bad weeks in a month before losing out on their monthly reward.

One very important thing to remember is that if your child misses out on their weekly or monthly reward, the rest of the family should receive theirs regardless. For example, if Johnny has chosen to have fish 'n' chips for his reward on Friday night but during the week he has misbehaved and had consequences placed on him then he would lose his reward. However, the rest of the family should not be punished alongside Johnny, so they would go ahead and have their fish 'n' chips. To some parents this sounds mean; however, you must remember that for the child with a behavioural disorder having the rest of the family miss out on their rewards is a reward in itself, simply because you also suffer.

Finally, remember your child should make a comprehensive list of all their rewards and choose a weekly reward at the start of the week. They can change their mind if it is not going to cause too many problems and they can add and subtract from their rewards list.

MYTHS

While I have heard many myths about parenting over the years, there are only two that I would like to deal with here. This is primarily because the following two myths appear to get unwarranted traction and are really quite troubling.

You should not discipline children

Remember that to discipline means to teach, to train, to guide and to set clear boundaries for acceptable behaviour. Of course children need this. Children raised in permissive homes where discipline is lacking or inconsistent experience many problems throughout their life. They have a tendency to not stick at anything – particularly when life gets tough. They are disobedient, oppositional, poor achievers, self-centred and can be very aggressive. Who wants to live in a world where this is a result of not disciplining children?

I have also been told a number of times by laypeople and confused parents alike that children with attention disorders like Attention–Deficit Hyperactivity Disorder (ADHD) or behavioural disorders like Oppositional Defiance Disorder (ODD) cannot learn appropriate behaviour. This is a fallacy, a myth that has no real evidence to support it. Commonly, children with ADHD or ODD will require a multimodal therapeutic approach that often includes the use of medication, social skills learning and a parent management training program. The simple fact is that children in these categories can learn, do learn and often respond very well to competent parenting.

You should relax discipline during difficulties

'We have recently separated and I have moved out of the family home with the children. It's been a difficult time for us all and especially the kids. I've been a little more relaxed on discipline and routines for the kids' sake – just to give them a chance to get used to the situation. It doesn't do them any harm to relax the rules a bit.'

I've heard this many, many times from separating or divorcing parents. Despite what you might think, relaxing or removing your children's normal routines and behavioural boundaries is not advantageous for your children. In fact, it can become a very real problem. Children need certainty in these times and the rules or boundaries and routines are just some of the ways in which children receive a very real sense of security. Removing routines and boundaries can leave your child feeling insecure, scared, confused and uncertain about what the future might hold. Furthermore, when parents relax the rules or the expectations of appropriate behaviour it can become very, very difficult to regain control over certain behaviours. This is because of the slippery slope that misbehaviour can take, which goes something like this. Parents feel sorry for their children and let some misbehaviours slide past without the usual consequences because they believe the 'misbehaviour' is in response to the separation or divorce. Then it happens again … and again. Then you notice the misbehaviour is becoming more serious and more problematic. Before long, little Johnny is misbehaving more and more and it becomes harder and harder for you to control the behaviour as he also becomes more argumentative and rebellious.

DEVELOPING THE DISCIPLINE PROGRAM HOMEWORK

1. List up to five of your child's behaviours that need to be modified on an A4 sheet of paper.
2. On the same A4 sheet of paper, list the corresponding consequences. Remember: one consequence per behaviour. Then laminate it.
3. Make a list of age-appropriate chores and, if finances permit, work out how much pocket money you are happy to pay your child and divide that total by the number of chores they might complete in a week. Remember to pay your child the allotted money once they have completed that chore.
4. Sit down and have a meeting with your child and discuss with them your concerns about their behaviour and how it *is* going to change. Show them the A4 sheet of paper containing the behaviours that are to change. Explain this in detail and provide examples and then move on to the consequences and explain how they will work.
5. Discuss with your child how they will now be doing chores around the house and ask for their input for a reasonable choice of chores.
6. Finally, inform your child they can 'earn' weekly and monthly rewards through modifying their behaviour and

then ask them to choose their rewards, in accordance with the directions outlined in this chapter.

A FINAL WORD

There are times when parenting can place enormous demands on parents; it can be one of the most difficult and stressful roles one has to contend with in adult life. Parents often feel pressured, as if they are supposed to know how to deal with every possible situation they encounter on the spot and always know exactly what to do, when to do it, how to do it, to never making a mistake and always being ready with the right answer at the right time. Throw a behavioural disorder into the mix and life for the parent can become unbearable. Parenting loses its joy and becomes a burden, and the hopes and dreams you had for your child the first time you held them seem to belong to another lifetime. But take heart, because the information presented in this book is designed to turn things around for you and your family. For instance, the information on active and reflective listening skills is designed to teach you how to reach in to your child's world, while the chapters on developing empathy and emotional intelligence are designed to help you build that close parent–child relationship you dreamed of. The information in this book will teach you how to respect your child, while at the same time it will teach your child how to respect you – and this is the foundation to a secure parent–child relationship and the foundation of any successful discipline program.

You may remember that in the introduction I urged you not to jump straight to the discipline program in an effort to get the upper hand over your child. If you have done this then you have missed the message of this book and are at risk of damaging the parent–child relationship. This discipline program is not about punishment; rather, through love, acceptance and clear boundaries, it places the power of parenting back into your hands. It is a discipline program that sustains itself and allows you to step back from the negative emotions and conflict that often take place. The discipline program teaches your child that they make choices about their behaviour and this is the foundation to learning self-control.

In my experience, parents are often full of self-doubt and fear failing or 'screwing up' the parenting skills and the discipline program as outlined in this book. But so what! So what if you make a mistake! So what if you don't get it right the first time! Get up, dust yourself off and try again. Keep on practising until you get it right. Compare the process to learning to drive a car. The first time you tried to drive a car you didn't just get in and drive it like you do today. It took time, effort, concentration and lots of practice before you could drive with confidence. How much more effort, concentration and practice is required for parenting and how much more important is parenting! Give yourself some time to learn and cut yourself some slack.

I wish you all well as you continue on with perhaps the most important job in your life – parenting.

Bibliography

Agerström, J., Möller, K., & Archer, T. 'Moral reasoning: the influence of affective personality, dilemma, content and gender', *Social Behavior and Personality*, 34.10, 1259–276.

Agrawal, H.R., Gunderson, J., Holmes, B.M., & Lyons-Ruth, K. (2004). 'Attachment studies with borderline patients: a review', *Harvard Review of Psychiatry*, 12, 94–104.

Ainsworth (nee Salter, 1940). *An Evaluation of Adjustment Based upon the Concept of Security*, Dissertation.

Ainsworth, M.D.S. (1963). 'The development of infant–mother interaction among the Ganda' in B.M. Foss (ed.), *Determinants of Infant Behavior*, 67–104, Wiley, New York.

Ainsworth, M.D.S. (1967). *Infancy in Uganda: Infant Care and the Growth of Love*, Johns Hopkins University Press, Baltimore.

Ainsworth, M.D.S. (1968). 'Object relations, dependency, and attachment: a theoretical review of the infant–mother relationship', *Child Development*, 40, 969–1025.

Ainsworth, M.D.S. (1989). 'Attachments beyond infancy', *American Psychologist*, 44, 709–16.

Ainsworth, M.D.S., & Bell, S.M. (1969). 'Some contemporary patterns in the feeding situation' in A. Ambrose (ed,), *Stimulation in Early Infancy*, 133–70, Academic Press, London.

Ainsworth, M.D.S., & Bell, S.M. (1970). 'Attachment, exploration, and separation: illustrated by the behavior of one-year-olds in a strange situation', *Child Development*, 41, 49–67.

Ainsworth, M.D.S., Bell, S.M., & Stayton, D. (1971). 'Individual differences in strange situation behavior of one-year-olds' in H. R. Schaffer (ed,), *The Origins of Human Social Relations*, 17–57, Academic Press, London.

Ainsworth, M.D.S., Bell, S.M., & Stayton, D. (1974). 'Infant–mother attachment and social development', in M.P. Richards (ed.), *The Introduction of the Child into a Social World*, pp. 99–135, Cambridge University Press, London.

Ainsworth, M.S., Blehar, M.C., Waters, E., & Wall, S. (1978). *Patterns of Attachment: A Psychological Study of the Strange Situation*, Erlbaum, Hillsdale, NJ.

Ainsworth, M.D.S., & Bowlby, J. (1991). 'An ethological approach to personality development', *American Psychologist*, 46, 331–41.

Ainsworth, M.D.S., & Wittig, B.A. (1969). 'Attachment and the exploratory behaviour of one-year-olds in a strange situation' in B.M. Foss (ed.), *Determinants of Infant Behaviour*, 113–36, Methuen, London.

Albiero, P., & Lo Coco, A. (2001). 'Designing a method to assess empathy in Italian children' in A. Bohart & D. Stipek (eds.), *Constructive and Destructive Behavior: Implications for Family, School & Society*, 205–23, American Psychological Association, Washington, DC.

Anderson, C.A., Sakamoto, A., Gentile, D.A., Ihori, N., Shibuya, A., et al. (2008). 'Longitudinal effects of violent video games on aggression in Japan and the United States', *Pediatrics,* 122.5, 1067–72.

Amendola, A.M., & Scozzie, S. (2004). 'Promising strategies for reducing violence', *Reclaiming Children and Youth,* 13:1, 51–3.

Armstrong, J.G., & Roth, D. M. (1989). 'Attachment and separation difficulties in eating disorders: a preliminary investigation', *International Journal of Eating Disorders*, 8, 141–55.

Arora, T., Hussain, S., Hubert Lam, K.B., Lily Yao, G., Thomas, G.N., & Taheri, S. (2013). 'Exploring the complex pathways among specific types of technology, self-reported sleep duration and body mass index in UK adolescents', *International Journal of Obesity*, 37, 1254–60.

Aviezer, O., Sagi, A., Resnick, G., & Gini, M. (2002). 'School competence in young adolescence: Links to early attachment relationships beyond concurrent self-perceived competence and representations of relationships', *International Journal of Behavioral Development,* 26, 397–409.

Balter, L. (1989). *Who's in Control? Dr. Balter's Guide to Discipline without Combat,* Poseidon Press, New York.

Bandura, A. (1974). 'Behavior theory and the models of man', *American Psychologist*, 859–69.

Barber, B.K. (1996). 'Parental psychological control: revisiting a neglected construct', *Child Development,* 67, 3296–319.

Barlow, D.H., & Durand, V.M. (2002). *Abnormal Psychology* (third ed.), Wadsworth Thomas Learning, Chapter 3, Belmont.

Barriga A.Q., Sullivan-Cosetti M., & Gibbs, J.C. (2009). 'Moral cognitive correlates of empathy in juvenile delinquents', *Criminal Behaviour and Mental Health,* 19, 253–64.

Batson, C.D., Batson, J.G., Griffitt, C.A., Barrientos, S., Brandt, J.R., Sprengelmeyer, P., & Bayly, M.J. (1989). 'Negative–state relief and the empathy–altruism hypothesis', *Journal of Personality and Social Psychology,* 56, 922–33.

Baumeister, R.F., Heatherton, T.F., & Tice, D.M. (1994). *Losing Control: How and Why People Fail at Self-regulation,* Academic Press, San Diego, CA.

Baumrind, D. (1991). 'Effective parenting during the early adolescent transition' in P.A. Cowan & E.M. Hetherington (eds), *Family Transitions,* 111–63), Erlbaum, Hillsdale.

Beaumiester, R.F., & Leary, M.R. (1995). 'The need to belong: desire for interpersonal attachments as a fundamental human motivation', *Psychological Bulletin,* 117, 497–529.

Baumrind, D., & Black, A.E. (1967). 'Socialization practices associated with dimensions of competence in preschool boys and girls', *Child Development,* 3, 291–327.

Bavolek, S.J. 1983 'Developing empathy in families', The Nurturing Parenting Programs. Family Development Resources, Inc. Park City UR.

Bell, S.M,, & Ainsworth, M.D.S. (1972). 'Infant crying and maternal responsiveness, *Child Development,* 43, 1171–90.

Benes, F.M. (2004). 'Konrad Lorenz, 1903–1989', *American Journal of Psychiatry,* 10, 1767.

Berthoz, S., Grèzes, J., Armony, J.L., Passingham, R.E., & Dolan, R.J. (2006). 'Affective response to one's own moral violations', *NeuroImage,* 31.2, 45–950.

Blair, J. (1997). 'Moral reasoning and the child with psychopathic tendencies', *Personality and Individual Difference,* 22, 731–9.

Blair, R.J.R., & Blair, K.S. (2009). 'Empathy, morality, and social convention: evidence from the study of psychopathy and other psychiatric disorders' in J. Decety & W. Ickes (eds.), *The Social Neuroscience of Empathy,* 139–52), MIT Press, Cambridge.

Bloomquist, M.L. (2006). *Skills Training for Children with Behavior Problems: Revised Edition: A Parent and Practitioner Guidebook.* The Guildford Press, New York.

Booth-Laforce, C., Oh, W., Kim, A.H., Rose-Krasnore, L., Rubin, K.H., & Burges, K. (2006). 'Attachment, self-worth, and peer-group functioning in middle childhood', *Attachment & Human Development*, 8, 309–25.

Block, J.H., Block, J., & Morrison, A. (1981). 'Parental agreement–disagreement on child-rearing orientations and gender-related personality correlates in children', *Child Development*, 52, 963–74.

Boon, H.J. (2007). 'Low- and high–achieving Australian secondary school students: their parenting, motivations and academic achievement', *Australian Psychologist*, 42, 212–25.

Bowlby, J. (1940). 'The influence of early environment in the development of neurosis and neurotic character', *International Journal of Psychoanalysis*, XXI, 1–25.

Bowlby, J. (1944). 'Forty-four juvenile thieves: their characters and home lives', *International Journal of Psychoanalysis*, XXV, 19–52.

Bowlby, J, (1949). 'The study and reduction of group tensions in the family', *Human Relations*, 2, 123–8.

Bowlby, J. (1951). *Maternal Care and Mental Health*, World Health Organization Monograph (Serial No. 2).

Bowlby, J. (1958). 'The nature of the child's tie to his mother', *International Journal of Psychoanalysis*, XXXIX, 1–23.

Bowlby, J. (1959). 'Separation anxiety', *International Journal of Psychoanalysis*, XLI, 1–25.

Bowlby, J. (1960). 'Grief and mourning in infancy and early childhood', *The Psychoanalytic Study of the Child*, VX, 3–39.

Bowlby, J, (1962a). 'Defences that follow loss: causation and function', unpublished manuscript, Tavistock Child Development Research Unit, London.

Bowlby, J. (1962b). 'Loss, detachment and defence', unpublished manuscript, Tavistock Child Development Research Unit, London.

Bowlby, J. (1969). *Attachment and Loss, Vol. 1: Attachment*, Basic Books, New York. Bowlby, J. (1973). *Attachment and Loss, Vol. 2: Separation*, Basic Books, New York.

Bowlby, J. (I980a). *Attachment and Loss, Vol. 3: Loss, Sadness and Depression*, Basic Books, New York.

Bowlby, J. (1988). *A Secure Base: Parent–child Attachment and Healthy Human Development*, Basic Books, New York.

Bowlby, J., Ainsworth, M., Boston, M., & Rosenbluth, D. (1956). 'The effects of mother–child separation: a follow-up study', *British Journal of Medical Psychology*, 29, 211–47.

Bowlby, J., & Parkes, C.M. (1970). 'Separation and loss within the family' in E.J. Anthony & C. Koupernik (eds), *The Child in His Family: International Yearbook of Child Psychiatry and Allied Professions*, 197–216), Wiley, New York.

Bretherton, I. (1992). 'The origins of attachment theory: John Bowlby and Mary Ainsworth', *Developmental Psychology,* 28, 759–75.

Brougham, R.R., Zail, C.M., Mendoza, C.M., & Miller, J.R. (2009). 'Stress, sex differences, and coping strategies among college students', *Current Psychology*, 28:85–97.

Burke, L.E. (1989). *Child Development* (fourth ed.), Allyn & Bacon, Needham Heights, Massachusetts.

Calamaro, C.J., Yang, K., Ratcllffe, S., & Chasens, E.R. (2012). 'Wired at a young age: the effect of caffeine and technology on sleep duration and body mass index in school-aged children', *Journal of Pediatric Health Care*, 26: 276–82.

Canetti, L., Kanyas, K., Lerer, B., Latzer, Y., & Bachar, E. (2008). 'Anorexia nervosa and parental bonding: the contribution of parent–grandparent relationships to eating disorder psychopathology', *Journal of Clinical Psychology*, 64, 703–16.

Carver, C.S., & Scheier, M.F. (1998). *On the Self-regulation of Behavior*, Cambridge University Press, New York.

Cassidy, J., Parke, R.D., Butkovsky, L., & Braungart, J.M. (1992). 'Family–peer connections: the roles of emotional expressiveness within the family and children's understanding of emotions', *Child Development, 63*, 603–18.

Chapman, G., & Campbell, R. (1997). *The Five Love Languages of Children,* Northfield Publishing, Chicago.

Chermak, G.D., & Musiek, F.E. (1992). 'Managing central auditory processing disorders in children and youth', *American Journal of Audiology* 1, 61–65.

Cohen, D., & Strayer, J. (1996). 'Empathy in conduct-disordered and comparison youth', *Developmental Psychology*, 32, 988–98.

Dads, M.R., Maujean, A., & Fraser, J.A. (2003). 'Parenting and conduct problems in children: Australia data and psychometric properties of the Alabama Parenting Questionnaire', *Australian Psychologist,* 38, 238–41.

Davis, M.H. (1994). *Empathy: A Social Psychological Approach*, Brown and Benchmark, Madison, Wisconsin.

Davis, M.H. (1996). *Empathy: A Social Psychological Approach*, Westview Press, Boulder.

Decety, J., & Jackson, P.L. (2004). 'The functional architecture of human empathy', *Behavioral and Cognitive Neuroscience Reviews*, 3, 71–100.

Decety, J., & Meyer, M. (2008). 'From emotion resonance to empathic understanding: a social developmental neuroscience account', *Development and Psychopathology*, 20, 1053–80.

Decovic, M. (1999). 'Parent adolescent conflict: possible determinants and consequences', *International Journal of Behavioral Development*, 23, 977–1000.

DeKemp, R.A., Overbeek, G., DeWied, M., Engels, R.C.M.E., & Scholte, R.H.J. (2007). 'Early adolescent empathy, parental support and antisocial behaviour', *The Journal of Genetic Psychology*, 168, 5–18.

Denham, S. (1998). *Emotional Development in Young Children*, Guildford Press, New York.

de Wied, M., Goudena, P.P., & Matthys, W. (2005). 'Empathy in boys with disruptive behaviour disorders', *Journal of Child Psychology and Psychiatry*, 46, 867–80.

Dobson, J. (1997). *The Heart of the Family,*. Garborgs Heart N Home. Minneapolis, MN.

Dumas, J.E., & Nilsen, W.J. (2003). *Abnormal Child and Adolescent Psychology,* 57, 62–63, 69, 74, Allyn & Bacon, Boston.

Dunn, J., Brown, J.R., & Maguire, M. (1995). 'The development of children's moral sensibility: individual differences and emotion understanding', *Developmental Psychology*, 31, 649–59.

Dwairy, M.A. (2008). 'Parental inconsistency versus parental authoritarianism: associations with symptoms of psychological disorders', *Journal of Youth and Adolescence*, 37: 616–26.

Dwairy, M.A. (2010). 'Parental inconsistency: a third cross-cultural research on parenting and psychological adjustment of children', *Journal of Child and Family Studies*, 19: 23–9.

Eisenberg, N. (2000). 'Emotion, regulation, and moral development', *Annual Review of Psychology*, 51, 665–97.

Eisenberg, M.E., & Aalsma, M.C. (2005). 'Bullying and peer victimization: position paper of the Society for Adolescent Medicine', *Journal of Adolescent Health*, 36, 88–91.

Eisenberg, N., & Fabes, R. A. (1998). 'Prosocial development' in W. Damon (series ed.) & N. Eisenberg (vol. ed.), *Handbook of Child Psychology: Vol. 3. Social, Emotional, and Personality Development* (5th ed., 701–78), Wiley, New York.

Ember, C.R., & Ember, M. (2005). 'Explaining corporal punishment of children: a cross-cultural study', *American Anthropologist*, 107, 609–19.

Esbjørn, B.H., Bender, P.K., Reinholdt-Dunne, M.L., Munck, L.A., & Ollendick, T.H. (2012). 'The development of anxiety disorders: considering the contributions of attachment and emotion regulation', *Clinical Child and Family Psychology Review*, 15, 129–43.

Eron, L.D., Huesmann, L.R., & Zeli, A. (1992). 'The role of parental variables in the learning of aggression' in Pepler, D.J., & Rubin, K.H (eds.), *The Development and Treatment of Childhood Aggression,* 169–79. Lawrence Erlbaum Associates Inc. New Jersey, Hillsdale.

Evans, I.M., Heriot, S.A., & Friedman, A.G. (2002). 'A behavioural pattern of irritability, hostility and inhibited empathy in children', *Clinical Child Psychology and Psychiatry*, 7, 211–24.

Feilhauer, J., Cima, M., Benjamins, C., & Muris, P. (2013). 'Knowing right from wrong, but just not always feeling it: relations among callous–unemotional traits, psychopathological symptoms, and cognitive and affective morality judgments in 8- to 12-year-old boys', *Child Psychiatry and Human Development*, 44, 709–16.

Feindler, E.L., & Starr, K.E. (2003). 'From steaming mad to staying cool: a constructive approach to anger control', *Reclaiming Children and Youth,* 12, 158–60.

Feshbach, N.D. (1978). 'Studies in empathic behavior in children' in B. Maher (Ed.), *Progress in Experimental Personality Research*. Vol. 8., Academic Place, New York.

Feshbach, N.D. (1987). 'Parental empathy and child adjustment/maladjustment', in N. Eisenberg & J. Strayer (eds), *Empathy and Its Development*, Cambridge University Press, New York.

Feshbach, N.D. (1997). 'Empathy: the formative years – implications for clinical practice' in A. Bohart & L. Greenberg (eds), *Empathy Reconsidered: New Directions in Psychotherapy*, 33–59, American Psychological Association, Washington, DC.

Finkenauer, C., Engles, R.C.M.E., & Baumeister, R.F. (2005). 'Parenting behaviour and adolescent behavioural and emotional problems: the role of self-control', *International Journal of Behavioral Development,* 29, 58–69.

Fonagy, P., Leigh, T., Steele, M., Steele, H., Kennedy, R., & Mattoon, G. (1996). 'The relation of attachment status, psychiatric classification, and response to psychotherapy', *Journal of Consulting and Clinical Psychology*, 64, 22–31.

Frey, K.S., Hirschstien, M.K., & Guzzo, B.A. (2000). 'Second step: preventing aggression by promoting social competence', *Journal of Emotional and Behavioural Disorders*, 8, 102–13.

Gallagher, E. (2004). 'Youth who victimise their parents', *Australian and New Zealand Journal of Family Therapy*, 25, 94–105.

Gallagher, E. (2004). 'Parents victimised by their children', *Australian and New Zealand Journal of Family Therapy*, 25, 1–12.

Gallo, D. (1989). 'Educating for empathy, reason and imagination', *The Journal of Creative Behaviour*, 23, 98–115.

Garber, J., & Flynn, C.A. (2001). 'Predictors of depressive cognitions in young adolescents.' *Cognitive Therapy and Research*, 25 353–76.

Geldard, K., & Geldard, D. (2004). *Counselling Children: A Practical Introduction.* (second ed.), Chapter 3, Sage Publications, London.

Goleman, D.P. (1995). *Emotional Intelligence: Why It Can Matter More Than IQ,* Bantam Books, New York

Goleman, D.P. (2005). *Working with Emotional Intelligence,* Bantam Books. Gossling, T. (2003). 'The price of morality: an analysis of personality, moral behaviour, and social rules in economic terms', *Journal of Business Ethics*, 45.1/2, 121–31.

Gottman, J., & Declaire, J. (1997). *Raising an Emotionally Intelligent Child,* Fireside, New York.

Gottman, J., & Silver, N. (2000). *The Seven Principles for Making Marriage Work,* Orion Books Ltd, London.

Greene, R.W., & Ablon, J.S. (2006). *Treating Explosive Kids: The Collaborative Problem-solving Approach,* The Guildford Press, New York.

Grill, R. (2005). *Parenting for a Peaceful World,* Longueville Media, New South Wales, Australia.

Gustavo C., Raffaelli, M., Laible, D.J., & Meyer, K.A. (1999). 'Why are girls less physically aggressive than boys? Personality and parenting mediators of physical aggression', *Faculty Publications,* Department of Psychology, paper 60.

Hagena, K.A., Ogdena, T., & Bjørnebekka, G. (2011). 'Treatment outcomes and mediators of parent management training: a one-year follow-up of children with conduct problems', *Journal of Clinical Child & Adolescent Psychology*, 40, 165–78.

Hagerty, B.M.K., Lynch-Sauer, J., Patusky, K.L., Bouwsema, M., & Collier, P. (1992). 'Sense of belonging: a vital mental health concept', Archives of *Psychiatric Nursing*, 6, 172–77.

Hardy, L.T. (2007). 'Attachment theory and reactive attachment disorder: theoretical perspectives and treatment implications', *Journal of Child and Adolescent Psychiatric Nursing*, 20.1, 27–39.

Hawes, D.J., & Dadds, M.R. (2007). 'Assessing parenting practices through parent-report and direct observation during parent-training', *Journal of Child and Family Studies, 15*, 555–68.

Hay, I., & Ashman, A.F. (2003). 'The development of adolescents' emotional stability and general self-concept: the interplay of parents, peers, and gender', *International Journal of Disability, Development and Education*, 50, 77–91.

Haynes, L.A., and Avery, A.W. (1979). 'Training adolescents in self-disclosure and empathy skills', *Journal of Community Psychology*, 26, 526–30.

Hoffman, M.L. (2000). *Empathy and Moral Development: Implications for Caring and Justice*, Cambridge University Press, New York.

Hoffman, M.L. (2001). 'Towards a comprehensive empathy-based theory of prosocial moral development' in Bohart, A.C. & Stipek, D.J. (eds), *Constructive & Destructive Behavior: Implications for Family, School and Society*, 61–86), American Psychological Association, Washington D.C.

Höfner, C., Schadler, C., & Richter, R. (2011). 'When men become fathers: men's identity at the transition to parenthood', *Journal of Comparative Family Studies*, 42.5, 669–86.

Hollin, C.R. (2003). 'Aggression replacement training: putting theory and research to work', *Reclaiming Children and Youth*, 12:3, 132–5.

Hymel, S. & Perren, S. (2015). 'Introduction to the special issue: moral disengagement and aggression in children and youth', *Merrill-Palmer Quarterly*, 61, 1–9.

Isley, S., O'Neil, R., Clatfelter, D., & Parke, R. D. (1999). 'Parent and child expressed affect and children's social acceptance and competence: modelling direct and indirect pathways', *Developmental Psychology*, 35, 547–60.

Jaursch S., Losel F., Beelmann A., & Stemmler M. (2009). 'Inconsistency in parenting between mothers and fathers and children's behavior problems', *Psychology in Erziehung and Unterricht*, 56:172–86.

Jenkins, J.M., Rasbash, J., & O'Connor, T. (2003). 'Family context factors that explain differential parent–child relationships', *Developmental Psychology, 39*, 99–119.

Karen, R. (1994). *Becoming Attached: First Relationships and How They Shape Our Capacity to Love,* Warner Books, New York.

Kaukiainen A., Bjorkqvist K., Lagerspetz K., Osterman K., Salmivalli C., Rothberg S., et al. 1999. 'The relationships between social intelligence, empathy, and three types of aggression', *Aggressive Behavior*, 25:81–9.

Kazdin, A.E. (1987). 'Treatment of antisocial behavior in children: current status and future directions', *Psychological Bulletin*, 102, 187–203.

Kinkenenauer, C., Engels, R.C.M.E., & Baumeister, R.F. (2005). 'Parenting behaviour and adolescent behavioural and emotional problems: the role of self-control', *International Journal of Behavioral Development,* 29, 58–69.

Kochanska, G., Clark, L.A., & Goldman, M.S. (1997). 'Implications of mothers' personality for their parenting and their young children's developmental outcomes', *Journal of Personality*, 65, 387–420.

Kochanska, G., Gross, J.N., Lin, M.H., & Nichols, K.E. (2002). 'Guilt in young children: development, determinants, and relations with a broader system of standards.' *Child Development*, 73, 461–82.

Kochanska, G., & Murray, K.T. (2000). 'Mother–child mutually responsive orientation and conscience development: from toddler to early school age', *Child Development*, 71, 417–31.

Kremen, A., & Block, J. (1998). 'The roots of ego-control in young adulthood: links with parenting in early childhood', *Journal of Personality and Social Psychology*, 75, 1062–75.

Kuehnle, K., & Ellis, T. (2002). 'The importance of parent–child relationships: what attorneys need to know about the impact of separation', *The Florida Bar Journal*, 76, 67–70.

Kullik, A., & Petermann, F. (2013). 'Attachment to parents and peers as a risk factor for adolescent depressive disorders: the mediating role of emotion regulation', *Child Psychiatry and Human Development*, 44, 537–48.

Lamb, M. (2004). *The Role of the Father in Child Development* (fourth ed.), John Wiley and Sons, Inc.

Lamb, M.E. (2005). 'Attachments, social networks, and developmental context', *Journal of Human Development*, 48, 108–12.

Lahey, B.B., Miller, T.L., Gordon, R.A., & Riley, A. (1999). 'Developmental epidemiology of the disruptive behaviour disorders' in H. Quay & A. Hogan (eds), *Handbook of the Disruptive Behaviour Disorders*, Academic Press, San Antonio.

Lahey, B.B., & Waldman, I.D. (2003). 'A developmental propensity model of the origins of conduct problems during childhood and adolescence' in B.B. Lahey, T.E. Moffitt, & A. Caspi (eds), *Causes of Conduct Disorder and Juvenile Delinquency*, 76–117, Guildford Press, New York.

Lemar, P.J. (2005). 'Authority and moral reasons: parenting style and children's perceptions of adult rule justifications', *International Journal of Behavioral Development,* 29, 265–70.

Lemmens, J.S., Valkenburg, P.M., & Peter, J. (2011). 'The effects of pathological gaming on aggressive behavior', *Journal of Youth and Adolescence*, 40, 38–47.

Lewis, M. & Johnson, R.J. (2005). 'The child and its family: the social network model', *Human Development*, 48, 8–27.

Lewis, M., Sullivan, M.W., Stanger, C., & Weiss, M. (1989). 'Self-development and self-conscious emotions', *Child Development* 60, 146–56.

Lindsey E.W., & Caldera Y.M. (2005). 'Interparental agreement on the use of control in childrearing and infants' compliance to mother's control strategies', *Journal of Infant Behavior and Development*, 28:165–78.

Loe, I.M., & Feldman, H.M. (2007). 'Academic and educational outcomes of children with ADHD,' *Journal of Paediatric Psychology*, 32, 643–54.

Main, M. (1996). 'Introduction to the special section on attachment and psychopathology: overview of the field of attachment', *Journal of Consulting and Clinical Psychology*, 64, 237–43.

Martin Maldonado-Duran, J., Lartigue, T., & Feintuch, M. (2000). 'Perinatal psychiatry: infant mental health interventions during pregnancy', *Bulletin of the Menninger Clinic*, 64.3, 317–43.

Mathes, E.W., Adams, H.E., & Davies, R.M. (1985). 'Jealousy: loss of relationship rewards, loss of self-esteem, depression, anxiety, and anger', *Journal of Personality and Social Psychology*, 42, 1552–61.

Maunder, R.G., and Hunter, J.J. (2008). 'Attachment relationships as determinants of physical health', *Journal of the American Academy of Psychoanalysis and Dynamic Psychiatry*, 36.1, 11–32.

Mayer, J.D., & Salovey, P. (1995). 'Emotional intelligence and the construction and regulation of feelings', *Applied and Preventive Psychology*, 4, 197–208.

Mayer, J.D., Salovey, P., & Caruso, D. (2000). 'The positive psychology of emotional intelligence', in R.J. Sternberg (ed.), *The Handbook of Intelligence*, 396– 420), Cambridge University Press, New York.

Mayer, J.D., Salovey, P., & Caruso, D. (2004). 'Emotional intelligence: theory, findings and implications', *Psychological Inquiry*, 15, 197–215.

Mayseless, O., Scharf, M., & Sholt, M. (2003). 'From authoritative parenting practices to an authoritarian context: exploring the person–environment fit', *Journal of Research on Adolescence*, 13, 427–56.

Mehrabian, A. (1997). 'Relations among personality scales of aggression, violence and empathy: validational evidence bearing on the risk of eruptive violence scale', *Aggressive Behavior*, 23, 433–45.

Miller, P., & Eisenberg, N. (1988). 'The relation of empathy to aggressive and externalizing/antisocial behaviour', *Psychological Bulletin*, 103, 324–44.

Miller, G.E., & Prinz, R.J. (1990). 'Enhancement of social learning: family interventions for childhood conduct disorder', *Psychological Bulletin*, 108, 291– 308.

Minton, C & Pasley, K. (1996). 'Father's parenting role: identity and father involvement', *Journal of Family Issues*, 17, 26–45.

Munezawa, T., Kaneita, Y., Osaki, Y., Kanda, H., Minowa, M., et al. (2011). 'The association between use of mobile phones after lights out and sleep disturbances among Japanese adolescents: a nationwide cross-sectional survey', *Sleep*, 34.8, 1013–20.

Nas, C.N., Brugman, D., & Koops, W. (2008). 'Measuring self-serving cognitive distortions with the How I Think Questionnaire', *European Journal of Psychological Assessment*, 24, 181–9.

Nichols, S. (2002). 'Norms with feeling: towards a psychological account of moral judgment', *Cognition*, 84(2), 221–36.

Omer, H. (2000). 'Parental Presence: reclaiming leadership in bringing up our children', Zeig, Tucker & Co. Phoenix AZ:

Oxford, M.L., Harachi, T.W., Catalano, R.F., Haggery, K.P., & Abbott, R.D. (2000). 'Early elementary school-aged child attachment to parents: a test of theory and implications for intervention', *Prevention Science*, 1, 61–9.

Parker, J., & Benson, M. (2004). 'Parent–adolescent relations and adolescent functioning: self-esteem, substance abuse and delinquency', *Adolescence,* 39, 519–31.

Pendry, P., & Adam, E.K. (2007). 'Associations between parents' marital functioning, maternal parenting quality, maternal emotion and child cortisol levels', *International Journal of Behavioural Development,* 31, 218–31.

Piaget, J. (1965). *The Moral Judgement of the Child*, The Free Press, New York.

Pickover, S. (2002). 'Breaking the cycle: a clinical example of disrupting an insecure attachment system', *Journal of Mental Health Counselling*, 24, 358–66.

Rehbein, F., Kleimann, M., & Mössle, T. (2010). 'Cyberpsychology, behavior and social networking prevalence and risk factors of video game dependency in adolescence: results of a German nationwide survey', *National Library of Medicine*, 13.3, 269–77.

Rogers, C.R. (1975). 'Empathic: an unappreciated way of being', *The Counselling Psychologist*, 5, 2–10.

Rowe, K., Rowe, K., & Pollard, J. (2004). 'Behaviour and auditory processing: building "fences" at the top of the "cliff" in preference to "ambulance services" at the bottom', Background paper to invited address presented at the ACER Research Conference, Adelaide SA, 24–26 October 2004.

Russell, A. (1997). 'Individual and family factors contributing to mothers' and fathers' positive parenting', *International Journal of Behavioral Development,* 21, 111–32.

Russel A., Russel G. (1994). 'Co-parenting early school-age children: an examination of mother–father interdependence within families', *Journal of Development Psychology*, 30:757–70.

Sadock, B.J., & Sadock, V.A (2003). *Synopsis of Psychiatry: Behavioral Sciences/ Clinical Psychiatry* (ninth ed.), 85–180, Lippincott Williams & Wilkins, Philadelphia.

Salisch, M.V. (2001). 'Children's emotional development: challenges in their relationships to parents, peers, and friends', *International Journal of Behavioral Development, 25*, 310–19.

Salovey, P., Hsee, C.K., & Mayer, J.D. (2001), *Emotions in Social Psychology: Essential Readings*, Psychology Press, Kentucky. I

Sandman, C.A., Davis, E.P., Buss, C., & Glynn, L.M. (2012). 'Exposure to prenatal psychobiological stress exerts programming influences on the mother and her foetus', *Neuroendocrinology*, 95, 7–21.

Shechtman, Z. (2002). 'Cognitive and affective empathy in aggressive boys: implications for counseling', *International Journal for the Advancement of Counseling*, 24, 211–22.

Simons, R.L., Johnson, C., & Conger, R.D. (1994). 'Harsh corporal punishment versus quality of parental involvement as an explanation of adolescent maladjustment', *Journal of Marriage and the Family*, 56, 591–607.

Simons, R.L., Leslie, G.S., Callie, H.B., Brody, G.H., & Cutrona, C. (2005). 'Collective efficacy, authoritative parenting and delinquency: a longitudinal test of a model integrating community- and family-level processes', *Criminology*, 43, 989–1029.

Slade, A. (2004). 'The move from categories to process: attachment phenomena and clinical evaluation', *Infant Mental Health Journal*, 5, 269–83.

Slade, A. & Cohen, L. J. (1996). 'Processes of parenting and the remembrance of things past', *Infant Mental Health Journal*, 17, 217–38.

Smetana, J.G., Campione-Barr, N., & Yell, N. (2003). 'Children's moral and affective judgments regarding provocation and retaliation', *Merrill-Palmer Quarterly*, 49.2, 209–36.

Soenens, B., Luyckx, K., Vansteenkiste., Duriez, B., & Goossens, L. (2008). 'Clarifying the link between parental psychological control and adolescents' depressive symptoms', *Merrill-Palmer Quarterly*, 54, 411–44.

Soenens, B., Vansteenkiste, M., & Luyten, P. (2010). 'Toward a domain-specific approach to the study of parental psychological control: distinguishing between dependency-oriented and achievement-oriented psychological control', *Journal of Personality*, 78, 217–56.

Sours, J.A. (1974). 'The anorexia nervosa syndrome', *International Journal of Psychoanalysis*, 55, 567–79.

Sours, J.A. (1980). *Starving to Death in a Sea of Objects: The Anorexia Nervosa Syndrome*, Jason Aronson, New York.

Spence, S.H. (2003). 'Social skills training with children and young people: theory, evidence and practice', *Child and Adolescent Mental Health, 8*, 84–96.

Stams, G.J., Brugman, D., Dekovic, M., van Rosmalen, L., van der Laan, P., & Gibbs, J.C. (2006). 'The moral judgment of juvenile delinquents: a meta-analysis', *Journal of Abnormal Child Psychology*, 34, 692–708.

Steinberg, L., Blatt-Eisengart, I., & Cauffman, E. (2006). 'Patterns of competence and adjustment among adolescents from authoritative, authoritarian, indulgent, and neglectful homes: a replication in a sample of serious juvenile offenders. *Journal of Research on Adolescence*, 16, 47–58.

Steinberg, L., Elman, J.D., & Mounts, N.S. (1989). 'Authoritative parenting, psychosocial maturity, and academic success among adolescents', *Child Development,* 60, 1424–36.

Stone, L.L., Otten, R., Janssens, J.M. A.M., Soenens, B., Kuntsche, E., & Engels, R.C.M.E. (2013). 'Does parental psychological control relate to internalizing and externalizing problems in early childhood? An examination using the Berkeley puppet interview', *International Journal of Behavioural Development*, 37, 309–18.

Tangney, J.P., Baumeister, R.F., & Boone, A.L. (1994). 'High self-control predicts good adjustment, less pathology, better grades, and interpersonal success', *Journal of Personality*, 72, 271–324.

Thomson, P. (2004). 'The impact of trauma on the embryo and fetus: an application of the Diathesis-Stress Model and the Neurovulnerability-Neurotoxicity Model', *Journal of Prenatal & Perinatal Psychology & Health,* 19.1, 9–63.

Thompson, K.L., & Gullone, E. (2003). 'Promotion of empathy and prosocial behaviour in children through humane education', *Australian Psychologist,* 38, 175–82.

Troisi, A., Massaroni, P., & Cuzzolaro, M. (2005). 'Early separation anxiety and adult attachment style in women with eating disorders', *The British Journal of Clinical Psychology*, 44, 89–97.

Tynjälä, J, Kannas, L., & Välimaa, R. (1993). 'How young Europeans sleep', *National Library of Medicine,* Health Education Research 8.1, 69–80.

Van den Bulck, J. (2007). 'Adolescent use of mobile phones for calling and for sending text messages after lights out: results from a prospective cohort study with a one-year follow-up', *Sleep*, 30.9, 1220–3.

Verlann, P., & Schwartzman, A.E. (2002). 'Mother's and father's parental adjustment: links to externalizing behaviour problems in sons and daughters', *International Journal of Behavioral Development,* 26, 214–24.

von Salisch, M. (2001). 'Children's emotional development: challenges in their relationships to parents, peers, and friends', *International Journal of Behavioral Development*, 25, 310–19.

Wang, Y.F. (2007). 'Attachment, filial piety, and mental health: testing cultural influence on the attachment–mental health link among Taiwanese high school students', Dissertation.

Webster-Stratton, C. & Reid, M.J. (2003). 'Treating conduct problems and strengthening social and emotional competence in young children: the Dina Dinosaur treatment program', *Journal of Emotional and Behavioral Disorders,* 11, 130–43.

Wei, H.T., Chen, M.H., Huang, P.C., & Bai, Y.M. (2012). 'The association between online gaming, social phobia, and depression: an internet survey', *BMC Psychiatry*, 92, 12–18.

Weiss, B., Dodge, K.A., Bates, J.E., & Pettit, G. S. (1992). 'Some consequences of early harsh discipline: child aggression and maladaptive social information processing style', *Child Development*, 53, 1321–5.

Weisz, J.R., Southam-Gerow, M.A., & McCarty, C.A. (2003). 'Control-related beliefs and depressive symptoms in clinic-referred children and adolescents: developmental differences and model specificity', *Journal of Abnormal Psychology*, 110, 97–109.

Widiger, T.A., & Samuel, D.B. (2005). 'Diagnostic categories or dimensions? A question for the *Diagnostic and Statistical Manual of Mental Disorders – Fifth Edition*', *Journal of Abnormal Psychology*, 114, 494–504.

Winsler A., Madigan A.L., Aquillino S.A. (2005). 'Correspondence between maternal and paternal parenting styles in early childhood', *Early Childhood Research Quarterly*, 20:1–12.

Wolfe, D.A., & McGee, R. (1994). 'Dimensions of child maltreatment and their relationship to adolescent adjustment', *Development and Psychopathology*, 6, 165–81.

Wood, J.J. (2006). 'Parental intrusiveness and children's separation anxiety in a clinical sample', *Child Psychiatry & Human Development*, 37, 73-87.

Wright, J., & Cullen, F. (2001). 'Parental efficacy and delinquent behaviour: do control and support matter?' *Criminology*, 39, 677–706.

Zahn-Waxler, C., & Radke-Yarrow, M. (1990). 'Origins of empathic concern', *Motivation and Emotion*, 14, 107–30.